T0095685

CHANTEYING
ABOARD AMERICAN SHIPS

Hands at a halyard on the bark *Alice*
(Mystic Seaport 1996.113.1.11)

CHANTEYING
ABOARD AMERICAN SHIPS

by Frederick Pease Harlow
Foreword by Glenn Grasso

MYSTIC SEAPORT · THE MUSEUM OF AMERICA AND THE SEA

Mystic Seaport
75 Greenmanville Ave., P.O. Box 6000
Mystic, CT 06355-0990

www.mysticseaport.org

© 1962 by Barre Publishing Company, Inc
© 2004 by Mystic Seaport Museum, Inc.
Foreword © 2004 by Glenn Grasso
All rights reserved. Published 2004
Second edition 2004

Printed in the United States of America
Cataloging-in-Publication Data

Harlow, Frederick Pease.
        Chanteying aboard American ships / by Frederick Pease Harlow ;
introduction by Glenn Grasso.—Mystic, Conn. : Mystic Seaport, c2004.
        p. : ill., music ; cm.
        Includes index.

        1. Folk-songs, English—United States—History and criticism. 2.
Sea songs—United States—History and criticism. I. Grasso, Glenn. II.
Title.

        ML3551.H28 2004

        ISBN 0-939511-01-0

To Elaine and Jim Tompkins

CONTENTS

LIST OF ILLUSTRATIONS

The photographs used to illustrate this book are from the collections of
Mystic Seaport and were taken on board the whaling bark *Charles W. Morgan* in 1916 and the American bark *Alice* during a voyage from New
York to New Zealand, probably in the 1890s.

FOREWORD

In March 1998 I wrote a brief biographical sketch of Frederick Pease Harlow for an encyclopedia of maritime literature. I relished the task with the confidence that only complete ignorance allows. It would be easy; I had already read Harlow's books, and a 200-word essay would be effortlessly accomplished in no time. Little did I know how that one assignment would launch a research project that is only now reaching fruition. *Chanteying Aboard American Ships* contained a one-line clue that led me on a what has been six-year mission to recover the tale of Frederick Pease Harlow, a sailor-turned-pioneer whose life story embodies America's maritime vitality and the westward expansion of the United States. This is indeed a rare book. Moreover, it only narrowly missed consignment to oblivion in the first place.

Frederick Pease Harlow is best known for *The Making of a Sailor, or Sea Life Aboard a Yankee Square-Rigger.* Editor George Francis Dow split the manuscript, originally titled *The Making of a Sailor: Chanteying on the Akbar,* into two parts. The first part, *The Making of a Sailor,* was published by the Marine Research Society in 1928. As Harlow wrote to his daughter Frances that year, he was confident that "there will be another book [of] all chanteys coming out next year. I am correcting the manuscript at odd times at the office."

Unfortunately, world travel and then World War II intervened. After nearly two decades, the *American Neptune* proposed serial publication of the chanteys and printed the first installment in April 1948. The second installment never followed. Between paper restrictions during the war and no publisher interested in a niche market afterwards, the manuscript languished in Walter Muir Whitehill's, and then Ernest Dodge's, desk at the *American Neptune* for years. Finally, Alden Johnson, the "imaginative proprietor of the Barre Gazette," stepped up to publish the book in its entirety, "which was what should have been done in the first place," Whitehill wrote in 1962. "Mr. Johnson is willing to publish a good maritime manuscript even if it has. . . a limited market."

Since its understated appearance in 1962, *Chanteying Aboard American*

Ships has proved itself a valuable, yet elusive and even enigmatic, firsthand source for nineteenth-century maritime music. Harlow's shipboard experience, careful eye for detail, expertise in square-rig mechanics, and clear descriptions illuminate how work songs actually worked. His three voyages—deepwater on the ship *Akbar*, coasting aboard the schooner *David G. Floyd*, and trading to Caribbean on the bark *Conquest*—articulate a full range of maritime experiences and the music surrounding each. Moreover, his eyewitness accounts of the African-Caribbean roots of sea music are singular. Finally, a lifelong enthusiasm for music of many styles ensured that his appraisal would be something more than mere nostalgia.

೪ ೫

A single line in Ernest Dodge's 1962 foreword to *Chanteying Aboard American Ships* reported: "Frederick Pease Harlow retired to Seattle where he died a few years ago." In fact, Harlow spent more than 60 years in Seattle. Nevertheless, this solitary piece of information offered a point of entry to the vital-statistic information I needed to begin a historical inquiry. Spring turned to summer, staff at the G.W. Blunt White Library at Mystic Seaport contacted the Seattle Public Library, and I finally had enough to write my encyclopedia entry. I knew there was more, though, and my interest was piqued by tantalizing references to an unpublished autobiography. Michael J. Mjelde saw it while writing *Glory of the Seas* (1970). Where was this document?

In March 1999, I arranged to travel ahead of a group of Williams College-Mystic Seaport Maritime Studies Program students to further explore the Seattle connection. After considerable detective work, I met an elderly gentleman named Tom Sandry. As a boy, he had known Harlow. Between his contacts and a considerable dose of luck (the researcher's best friend), I found myself several telephone calls later talking to Harlow's granddaughter, Elaine Eberle Tompkins. Mrs. Tompkins graciously invited me into her home, and I found myself face-to-face not only with the unpublished autobiography, but also with boxes and boxes of materials. She had inherited all of her grandfather's papers, including dozens of letters, photographs, journals and logbooks, and manuscripts. Frederick Pease Harlow's handwritten journal was among the treasures.

Elaine and her husband Jim, a retired U.S. Navy captain, were lovely people. After our first meeting, we exchanged telephone calls and Christmas cards. In 2000, the Tompkinses donated four models built by Harlow to Mystic Seaport: models of the ship *Akbar*, bark *Conquest*, ship *Great Admiral*, and ship *Glory of the Seas*. The original figurehead from the *Great Admiral* is already in the Museum's collection, and the *Glory* model is particularly interesting. It was built out of pieces of the original ship that Harlow collected from the Seattle beach where the vessel was burned.

In 2002, the graduate school at the University of New Hampshire generously funded a research trip so I could further explore Seattle archives and visit Jim and Elaine Tompkins. Over the course of two days we shared some very pleasant meals, relaxed on their lovely, west-facing deck, and talked about their family history and remembrances of Harlow and his wife, Gertrude. I read in the journal and photocopied the typescript of the autobiography. We talked about plans for the future of the papers. I emphasized their historical significance to maritime scholars and the need for archival preservation, but we left the conversation unfinished.

To my great surprise and delight, I received a message in the fall of 2002 that the collection had arrived in Mystic. It seems that the intrepid Jim and Elaine Tompkins drove across the country with the collection and donated it to Mystic Seaport! We had discussed this option among many others during my visit, but we never reached any firm conclusions. The Tompkinses decided to take action. There were some last-minute complications, but in the end, the couple deposited six boxes—the entirety of the collection—in the safety of the vault at the G.W. Blunt White Library. The certificate of gift arrived just before the New Year.

In 2003, UNH again generously provided fellowship funding for me to catalog the collection for the library. Working with Library Director Paul O'Pecko, Manuscript Archivist Leah Prescott, and the rest of the Library staff

Harlow, Williams, Frank, Archie, and Sprague (Jim Dunn) of the ship *Akbar*, 1877 (Mystic Seaport 2004.11.1)

xvii

was a great pleasure, one second only to working with the materials themselves. Cataloging the collection has been richly rewarding personally, and it has considerably enhanced our knowledge of Harlow and how he wrote his books.

ᘒᘓ ᘒᘓ

Much is certain. Frederick Pease Harlow was born on 12 December 1856, in Mount Morris, Illinois, to Frances Ann Harlow and the Reverend William T. Harlow. He grew up in Illinois until age 10, when he, brother Will, and their mother traveled back East. After living for a time with an East Boston uncle and cousins, the family returned to their ancestral home: Duxbury, Massachusetts. Next, they moved to Bristol, then Newport, Rhode Island.

Fred's three older brothers were sailors, and he was determined to follow in their footsteps. He sailed to Australia and Asia aboard the *Akbar*, to Georgetown, D.C., on the schooner *David G. Floyd*, and to Barbados on the bark *Conquest*. Harlow quit the sea when the *Conquest's* drunken captain almost ran the vessel aground off Chatham, Massachusetts, on the return passage. He then headed west, worked as a book salesman for the Methodist Book Concern of Chicago and, after two years, entered a service with strong similarities to maritime culture. He literally "rode shotgun" as an express messenger to protect money and cargo entrusted to Wells, Fargo & Company.

After a decade, the itinerant life wore on Harlow. Bandits, cowboys, and drunken railroad brakemen shot him at him. He witnessed Apache attacks and foiled train robberies. In New Mexico, he narrowly

Harlow (seated at left), his dog, and other railroad messengers, New Mexico, ca. 1885. (Mystic Seaport 2004.11.2)

avoided a confrontation with Jesse James's gang. The train he rode wrecked four times. After surviving the fourth wreck, he nervously awoke every time the "engineer put on the brakes going down a grade." Transferring to an office job, he eventually relocated to Portland, Oregon, to work for the Northern Pacific Express Company. After a few uneventful years in Portland, Harlow again transferred, this time to the city that would be the geographic terminus of his life: Seattle, Washington.

Harlow moved to Seattle in 1890, the year the census bureau declared the American frontier closed. Even more fortuitous was the timing of his move to Seattle. He arrived a mere seven months after that city's "great fire," as the city was rebuilding, poised to become the premier deepwater port in the Pacific Northwest. The city's rebirth meant opportunity. Harlow began shipping salmon, using his position as express agent to coordinate fish companies with rail transportation. He became express agent for multiple companies. In the city directory, his name and businesses took up more and more space throughout the 1890s. In a more personal development, he married Lottie Gertrude Gilleland of Seattle on Valentine's Day, 1898. They had one daughter, Frances Ann Harlow.

Seattle's growth continued to provide opportunities for Harlow. He began a cement contracting company to pave the city's sidewalks. He was a salesman for the Port Orchard Clay Company, helped found and was treasurer of the Occidental Fish Company, sold lumber, oversaw the repair of the schooner *William Nottingham*, and worked for the Puget Sound Navigation Company.

Despite largely holding desk jobs, Harlow was a traveler at heart, and his wanderlust remained a potent force throughout his life. He and brother Will went to the Chicago world's fair in 1893. In 1897, they bicycled from Portland to Seattle, and later through Yellowstone Park. After his retirement in 1933, Fred and Gert drove around the country. Gertrude wanted to imitate her sister, so she took the wheel for the entire trip. After nearly two years on the road, the Harlows embarked on a voyage around the world by steamer. Leaving from Laguna Beach, California, on 1 April 1935, they crossed the Pacific and Indian Oceans, went through the Suez Canal into the Mediterranean Sea, and crossed the Atlantic Ocean. Passing through the Panama Canal, they returned to Southern California before driving home to Seattle. "We were indeed fortunite [sic] in having perfect weather for all places of interest," wrote Harlow. "I doubt if we had ten days of rain for the entire trip." Even luckier, they enjoyed one of the last opportunities to see the prewar world of 1935-36.

Harlow's round-the-world trip marked another significant passage. Crossing the Atlantic aboard the steamer *Britannic*, he finished something started 61 years earlier. April 30, 1936, he wrote, was "a red letter day for me, having completed a circle around the world at Lat. 40, N. Long 67, W. . . . With less than 2 degrees to go we crossed the path of that of the 'Akbar' in 1875." Six decades after he began, Frederick Pease Harlow had finally circumnavigated the globe.

Harlow returned to Seattle and penned his memoirs. He never stopped trying to find a publisher for the memoirs and for his long-neglected book of chanteys. He passed his time by following World War II, listening to baseball games on the radio, building ship models, collecting more sea music, and playing the fiddle. Once he helped organize a chantey concert with the University of Washington Glee Club. He continually revised his memoirs and stayed involved in Seattle's maritime community as it grew to international prominence. However, when he died three months shy of his 96th birthday on 10 September 1952, *Chanteying Aboard American Ships* remained unpublished.

෧෬ ෬෧

Working with the Harlow collection has increased our knowledge of his life and works exponentially. Nevertheless, there are aspects of Harlow's creative processes that bear further examination. Most first-person narratives imply an intrinsic candor. However, most first-person narratives are also filled with inconsistencies between the historical record and the events as written by their authors. The premier example, in Harlow's case, is his seagoing career. It is now clear that Harlow first sailed on the *Akbar* to Australia and Asia. Upon his return, he joined the *Floyd* and sailed to Georgetown, and his last voyage was aboard the *Conquest. The Making of a Sailor* is a tale of rising action, beginning with a father's reluctant permission to go to sea, then chronicling a short coasting voyage to the Chesapeake, and finally leading to the climax of the book—an identity-forming deepwater voyage to Australia and back. Harlow's journal and letters tell a different story: one of a seafaring life that begins with a deepwater voyage as a greenhand aboard the *Akbar*, continues with a coasting voyage as an interlude, and concludes with a trip to Barbados.

This discovery hardly indicts Harlow's works or their worth. Instead, it leads to a richer understanding of both. In fact, it moves Harlow from a simple chronicler and collector to a writer of maritime literature. His works, like all great literature, are complex blends of experience and embellishment in order to tell a tale. Along with a deep knowledge of maritime topics and habits, he used his substantial maritime experience to create a complex admixture. As well as evaluating Frederick Pease Harlow as a musicologist and narrative writer, we must also evaluate him as an artist.

෧෬ ෬෧

When I began my search, little did I know just how long and rich a life Harlow's would turn out to be. Reflecting the life he lived, Harlow's writing has contributed immeasurably to our knowledge of sea music, maritime culture, square-rigged sail, and shipboard life. As a writer and model-builder, Harlow's attention to detail shines. Above all, Frederick Pease Harlow was a collector. He saved postcards of ships that visited the Seattle waterfront and sermons his father delivered in the 1830s. He made long lists of vessels wrecked on the Pacific Northwest coast. Fortunately, he was a collector who could read and write musical notation. To augment his personal knowledge of sea music, he sought out songs through research and correspondence. Moreover, with his critical eyes and ears informed by his seafaring experience, he provided astute commentary on many sources of maritime music and culture. Harlow was a collector, educator, and conservator of the genre, and *Chanteying Aboard American Ships* is his paramount collection. Indeed, it has proven to be influential far beyond the original number printed. Like Alden Johnson over four decades ago, Mystic Seaport is willing to risk publishing books for a niche market. *Chanteying Aboard American Ships* is among the most elusive and difficult-to-find books of sea music. It is at last receiving the attention it deserves.

Glenn Grasso
University of New Hampshire

Frederick Pease Harlow, ca. 1925. (Courtesy Glenn Grasso)

Heaving the capstan on the bark *Alice*
(Mystic Seaport 1996.113.1.29)

The Chantey

When manning the windlass,
Or setting the sails,
To rouse home the fore sheet
In stiff blowing gales,
You chantey and sing with
A chorus so strong,
That one man's worth four
As the ship bowls along.

A CHANTEY (pronounced "Shanty") is a song sung by sailors aboard ship while doing various kinds of manual work of a heavy nature. This, to the landsman, may seem ridiculous, but, notwithstanding, the right song at the right time, with sailors, accomplished what otherwise could not have been done.

Chanties were principally used in the merchant service and seldom, if ever were heard in the navy. The word is probably taken from the French *chanter,* to sing. It is a combination of chant and song; i.e., the chanteyman led off with a solo, for a line or two, when it was taken up by the crew in a chorus. So common were the chanties in the '70s, that they were sung on all square-riggers, even in brigs and topsail schooners; and instead of confining themselves to the old verses and words, the sailors were privileged to sing any words that would rhyme. Consequently the riffraff of creation felt at liberty to sing and use words of their own choice, rhyme or no rhyme with the result that they frequently had vulgar songs so vile and rotten that no one ever attempted to

1

set them to music and if ever published it would surely be a penitentiary offence. The sailors' words in the chantey are not unlike the Erie Canal mule drivers' cursing and swearing to his team. Both get results, but to say the least are entirely uncalled for and quite unnecessary.

Have you ever listened, on a moonlit summer evening, to the sound of the oars and the splash of water, as the oarsman pulled his boat in the stillness of the night and just far enough away for you to catch an occasional word as he talked to a companion, finally breaking out in a low, sweet song which gradually became more distinct as the boat came nearer to the shore, and within speaking distance the music ceased and you wished for just one more strain — is there anything sweeter? There can be no comparison with the music coming over the water on a balmy day, when you hear a rousing chorus of men's voices as they chantey, while heaving up anchor on a packet ship lying in the stream; just far enough away to catch the strain; sometimes stronger and then again fainter as the wind wafts it in another direction, only to be returned again much stronger as the ship is being warped to the dock. When once heard, it leaves an impression never to be forgotten.

As the ship draws nearer you hear the leading chanteyman sing his solo, of a line or two, and before the last word is fairly out, the crew break in with a rousing chorus that none but men can quite equal. Verse after verse and song after song is sung. No matter if the sailor be an American, Englishman, Norwegian, or Frenchman, all know the chorus and come in with a will.

Many a chanteyman with a good voice but dull of comprehension would string out a chantey by repeating every line, using words with no meaning and sometimes without regard to rhyme or metre. But if he were original, he would make up verses as he sang, bringing in incidents of the voyage in such a vivid way that the crew redoubled their efforts at the capstan bars or ropes, thus getting more pleasure from the work and keeping them in a contented mood. A good chanteyman, therefore, was often paid more than the common sailor for his ability to get work out of the men; which was sometimes very much needed in ports where the crew were obliged to work the cargo.

As the ship neared the dock one could see the men walk around the capstan while they sang *Heave Away, Johnny,* and could pick out

"English Jack," by his guernsey sweater and Scotch cap; "Dutch Herman," in his red shirt; "Irish Patsy," in his dungaree overalls and the "Yank" with his sleeves rolled up and the neck of his woolen shirt unbuttoned and thrown back, exposing a chest sunburned from a tropical sea, as, in fact they all were. The look of pleasure might be seen on their faces as they neared the dock and looked wistfully ashore, as much as to say, "We'll soon be with you and forget the trials of a ten month's voyage."

After the ship was made fast fore and aft, the last order from the mate was, "Man the pumps, lads." By this time the runners from the sailor boarding houses had been aboard and supplied the members of the crew with plenty of poor whiskey. Some were good natured, while others showed ill temper and were inclined to be mean as they thought of their independence near at hand. When the pump brakes were shipped into the brake beams of the pumps for the last time, they were still in condition to sing, whether the voyage had been a tough one or not. The chanteyman would jump on top of the brake beams holding on to the chain topsail sheets with his hands, and if able to stand would tread down on the brakes with his feet as the pumps were being worked by the balance of the crew and start, *Leave Her Johnny, Leave Her.*

If the pumps did not suck by the time the chantey was ended, one might see an occasional sailor, who had imbibed too freely, desert his post at the pumps and walk with an important step to the forecastle where he would tell you that he was part owner of the ship and he didn't see why he should work any longer, there being enough to do the work without him. Some had already changed their clothes and were ready to go with the boarding house runners who were doing their best to spirit the crew away. The officers by this time had the work in hand and would finish with the help of the boys, without making any trouble, and so, with blinded eyes, would let the crew go, and so the voyage came to an end.

When the ship was ready for sea again, a new crew was shipped and the new chanteyman as a rule had his own favorite songs with entirely different words from those sung on the voyage just ended. While he might use different words for his solo, the air and the chorus were the same, for chanties have been sung from time immemorial. One writer says chanties can be traced as far back as the year 1450.

There are four different kinds of chanties, which may be classed as follows: — The CAPSTAN, LONG DRAG, SHORT DRAG, and HAND OVER HAND.

The CAPSTAN CHANTEY was sung while weighing anchor, hoisting topsails, loading or unloading cargo, warping, or any kind of work requiring a song at the capstan or windlass.

These songs are more harmonious than any of the others and in early days, when a packet ship had anchored in the stream, just in from a foreign port, and was getting ready to warp into the dock, while heaving up the anchor the chorus of the chantey could be heard by the people on shore, who gathered in large numbers on the pier head to listen to such chanties as *Rio Grande, Sacramento, Shenandoah,* etc. But today, everything is as silent as a man o' war, for the sailor hardly knows a chantey when he hears it. Steam has replaced the brawn and muscle of the old school, for every day our old sailing vessels are being fitted and equipped, one by one, with modern improvements. Steam and electric winches are being installed in our modern sailing vessels for hoisting sails and cargo. The gypsy winch, for handling cargo, is already out of date and in another decade the common sailor will be insulted if the mate dares to issue an order to "Man the capstan."

The LONG DRAG CHANTEY is a hoisting chantey and was sung at the topsail halliards as the yard was being mastheaded by hand. It required "A long pull, a strong pull and a pull all together."

One of the best known chanteys for the topsails is *Whiskey.* There was always a smile on the old salt's face when this song was started. It was usually the first pulling chantey sung by a new crew and as many of them often came aboard drunk, either from choice or from being "shanghaied," shipmates would see the comical side of the condition under which they came on board and no matter how hard their heads ached they were always there with a strong chorus. The remembrance of a jolly good time ashore helped to "drive dull care away," and so made *Whiskey* one of the most popular chanties.

The chanteyman led off in his solo, marking the time for the pull.

THE CHANTEY

Chanteyman:	Oh, *Whiskey* is the *life* of man.
Chorus:	Oh, *Whiskey,* *Johnny.*
Chanteyman:	It *always* was since *time* began.
Chorus:	Oh *Whiskey* for my *Johnny.*

The capstan chanties usually have two choruses, a short and a long one. The long drag chanties have two choruses, but they are generally short and of the same length as the solo. This chanty was not confined to the topsails alone for it was also sung in any heavy work requiring a long hoist.

The SHORT DRAG CHANTEY was usually sung in a gale of wind hauling aft the sheet of the courses, boarding the main tack, or hauling out the bowline. It has one solo and a chorus, but there was no pulling until the last word was sung and then all hands exerted themselves as one, in a mighty pull.

Chanteyman:	Oh, haul, haul away, come haul and sway together.
Chorus:	Away, haul away, haul away, *Joe!*

To appreciate this chanty fully one must actually see or take part in the work. To stand knee deep in water at the lee scuppers, the seas breaking over the vessel as she gathers headway under the new stretch of canvas; with decks awash and the whole crew stringing out with feet braced, holding the fore sheet with a deathlike grip in an effort to gain, foot by foot, the necessary amount of the sheet from the balloon-like sail which is straining and groaning to be free from the bolt-ropes and lash the waves with its ribbons as the good ship throws herself into a head sea: that is life on the ocean wave.

The HAND OVER HAND CHANTEY was sung while hoisting light sails with two or three men on the halliards. They all sang together as they hoisted hand over hand. Light sails were not confined, however, to this style of chantey, for they were often hoisted with a solo and chorus. The best known hand over hand chantey is *The Drunken Sailor (Early in the Morning)*.

At the beginning of the nineteenth century chanties in minor keys prevailed. The sadder the words the more mournful the tune. These doleful songs gradually gave place to something more lively, and in the days of the old packet ships, loading cotton before the Civil War, we found the southern negro chanteying, while screwing cotton in place in the hold of vessels, with such songs as *We're All Surrounded.*

WE'RE ALL SURROUNDED

Martha wept and Mary cried.
>*We're all surrounded.*
That good ole man he up and died.
>*We're all surrounded.*
Carry the news,
>*Carry the news to Mary.*
Carry the news, for
>*We're all surrounded.*

6

The negroes on the plantations sang an altogether different song. Their songs were of a melody in which harmony predominated. Not so with the sailor. He sang his song for a different method — to mark time, for concerted action, and usually the chorus was sung in unison by the members of the crew. The southern negroes are not gifted to sing a chorus in unison and consequently they employed their harmonious faculties on the chantey, with the result that the whites soon began to imitate them, picking up heavier choruses until the chanties reached their zenith in the 1870's. Then steam began blowing out the cylinder heads of the chanteyman and in the 1880's, a vessel without a donkey engine aboard was away behind the times. The anchor windlass and capstans were connected with steam and the poor sailor and his chanties began drifting hopelessly down the bay and now are far out to sea, hull down — yes! Only topgallant sails showing. In fact, now one scarcely ever hears the "sing out" from members of the crew, when pulling in the slack of a line — the spring, or bow line, as the ship is being moved ahead or astern, while moored at the dock.

Sailors were so accustomed to singing out when there was a pull to be made, that I have actually heard an old sailor give a "Yo-ho-hip" when pulling on his sea boots.

A timber was launched aft or a heavy object was always moved to the cry of "Yo-ho-*hip!*" "Oh, *launch* him!" "Oh, *roll* him, etc. A haul on a brace was made to the cry of, *"Away, hey!" Away, hey!"* "Oh, *ho- boys!"* "A-*hoy-yah!"* Oh, *square him"* etc.

The pull on the halliards was usually more musical, according to the man singing out. This was a long hoist and the cry started in a monotone, gradually becoming more musical as the chanteyman warmed up and finally bursting forth in a chantey. No two men have the same cry, as a rule. Some began with a falsetto, blending into the natural voice, and others were just the reverse. Some cries end in a rising inflection, while others take the falling. The best cries were in the minor key. But I know of no way to write those which take the falsetto and should I attempt to describe the tone I fear my best efforts would fail to give it justice.

In lifting or moving an object. The pull comes on the accent with a blast of the breath.

A SHORT CRY OR SING OUT

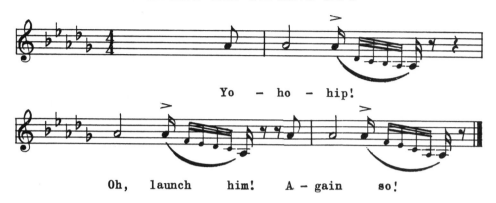

Yo - ho - hip!

Oh, launch him! A - gain so!

Yo ho hip!
Oh, launch him!
Again so!

WEATHER MAIN BRACE

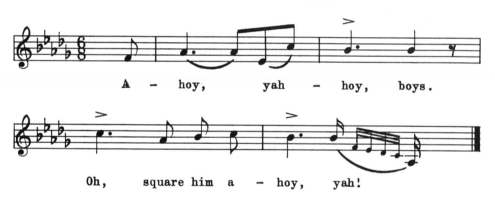

A - hoy, yah - hoy, boys.

Oh, square him a - hoy, yah!

Ahoy, yah-hoy, boys.
Oh, square him ahoy, yah!

TOPSAIL HALLIARDS
LONG DRAG

A - way, hey, oh, raise him a -

8

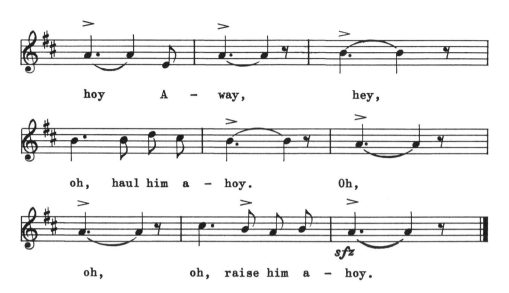

hoy   A - way,   hey,

oh,   haul him a - hoy.   Oh,

oh,   oh, raise him a - hoy.

Away, hey, oh, raise him ahoy.
Away, hey, oh haul him ahoy.
Oh, oh, oh, raise him ahoy.

A WALK AWAY

A - way – hey – a – a – ay.

Away hey-a-a-ay.

CALLING THE WATCH

Hay–a–a you sleep-ers,   eight bells are gone!

Hay-a-a you sleepers,
Eight bells are gone!

9

This is sung most vigorously by pounding on the fo'c'sle door with one's fist or belaying pin, usually to the time of the yell, and then, in an authoritative voice, "Tumble out you starbolines! Shake a leg! Shake a leg!"

These short cries were not termed chanties. But a pull with the sailors without a cry or "sing out", was like a team of horses pulling a heavy load under the guidance of a bank clerk.

When one considers that the sailor was made to sing out when pulling a rope; that he must creep before he walks and walk before he runs; his first attempt to imitate his shipmates was to sing out on some short pull where he would not be seen or heard. Gaining confidence in his ability he would practice further on the fore sheet while helping the cook take in the slack as the yards swung around, and while the clew of the sail was being hauled aft with a brisk walk along the deck; he then felt entitled to sing out his "Away-hey-a-a-ay."

This was where the boy shone. He had no fear that the "doctor" (the cook) would call him down when he led off in a sing out; whereas, at the braces or halliards, he would be entirely out of place, for some "old salt" would gruffly tell him, "Your place is behind the rest, ready for a turn."

Singing out at the braces or in any other form of pulling, was always done by the chanteyman starting to cry out, and never by more than one man at a time.

In issuing an order for a pull on the braces, the officer in charge of the watch gave the command, "There, give a small pull on the weather main brace." Whereupon some member of the crew answered, "A small pull on the weather main brace, sir," and the rest of the watch would follow aft with a rush to the weather rail, and the click of the patent blocks would ring out to the cry of, "Away-hey, boys." When the yard was squared in enough the officer would say, "That'll do the main, Belay!" "Belay, sir," was answered and the boy, who was always stationed behind the others, threw a turn over the belaying pin, singing out, "*All* fast!" If the rest of the yards needed bracing, they were taken in turn — lower topsail, upper topsail, topgallant, and royal yards.

As the officer of the deck stood in his exalted position at the weather side of the quarter deck, with a watchful eye on the weather, to take advantage of any change of wind, so the sailor aspired to be leader of the watch, by being the first to lay hands on the rope, or brace, taking his position at the fall, next to the block, and with a hearty cry, giving the time of the haul to the balance of the watch who were stringing out behind him and silently pulling to his music.

If any pull was done without a cry, which sometimes happened at night, because of the drowsiness of the watch who did not arouse themselves sufficiently to the occasion, or did not sing out as quickly as the officer of the deck thought they should, he would soon inform them, with an oath, that he wanted to hear a cry from some one, if it was nothing more than, "Go to h--l," for he wanted to know just what was being done.

These short cries were not of stereotyped form. Each sailor had a peculiar yell of his own, and so familiar were they with each other's cry that one might lie in his bunk and although not able to see the work being done, could tell by the sound the nature of the work and who was giving the cry.

Sweating a brace on the bark *Alice* (Mystic Seaport 1996.113.1.62)

Chanteying On The Akbar

THE SHIP *Akbar*, of Peabody's Australian Line, was about 1000 tons burden, carried three royal yards and was hemp rigged. She had a bell shaped bow, showing that she would be a comfortable and dry ship. She lay at Lewis Wharf, Boston, advertised to sail for Melbourne and Sidney.

Early in December 1875, lines were cast off and she was towed to an anchorage at Nantasket Roads awaiting a rising barometer.

Friday is a Jonah for most ships, but about ten o'clock in the morning the captain came off in the tugboat *Elsie* and as he came alongside he called, "Man the windlass, Mr. Burris, and get under way at once." "Aye, aye, sir! Man the windlass," called the mate. The men at work at their respective jobs were not loath to quit and hurried to the forecastlehead with a glad, "Man the windlass, sir!"

The brakes were shipped and the men in a cheerful mood went to work with a will, while Andy, Alonzo and I took care of the cable as it came over the windlass. The music of the pawls dropping — clank, clank, clank — was broken by Jerry starting a chantey, the first one sung aboard the ship. Up and down worked the windlass brakes in time to his solo and before the last word of the solo was fairly sung, the crew, in their eagerness, broke in on the chorus with a rousing "Heave away, my Johnnies."

Jerry had a fine voice and started the chantey in a clear tone which rang out beyond comparison in his crescendoes.

13

HEAVE AWAY MY JOHNNIES (WE'RE ALL BOUND TO GO)

CAPSTAN

We're all bound for Liv-er-pool, I heard the cap-tain say; Heave a-way my John-nies heave a-way, ... Oh! There we'll have a bul-ly time with Nel-lie and Ju-lie and May; Heave-a way my John-ny boys, We're all bound to go.

We're all bound for Liverpool,
    I heard the captain say;
Heave away my Johnnies, heave away.
Oh! There we'll have a bully time
    With Nellie and Julie and May;
Heave away my Johnny boys,
    We're all bound to go.

As I was walking out one day,
    Down by the Clarence Dock,

14

I overheard an emigrant,
    Conversing with Mister Tapscott.

"Good morning, Mister Tapscott!"
    "Good morning, sir!" said he.
"Oh! have you got any packet ship,
    To carry me over the sea?"

"Oh! yes, indeed! I've got packet ships;
    They sail in a day or two.
I've got the *Josie Walker*
    Besides the *Kangaroo*."

"The *Josie Walker* sails Friday,
    Her hatches all ready to seal;
With all, four hundred emigrants,
    And a thousand bags o' mail."

"You'll not sail me on the *Walker* ship,
    I'll not climb over the rail;
To hell with you and the *Walker* ship,
    And your thousand bags o' mail."

Some say we're bound for Liverpool;
    Some say we're bound for France;
But now we're bound for Melbourne town,
    To give the girls a chance.

The clouds are floating steady;
    The wind is blowing free;
We'll heave her short and be ready
    For the towboat to take us to sea.

Tapscott, of the foregoing chantey, in the early 1850's was one of the wealthy shipowners of Liverpool. His vessels were noted for strict discipline, as well as cruelty to the crew. His *Josie Walker* was an emigrant ship trading between Liverpool and New York. Her voyages to and from the Continent were marked by unheard of cruelties, stories of which spread along the waterfront, and the ship was known to all sailors as "Tapscott's *Josie Walker.*" The mention of this "hell ship" stopped many a good sailor from shipping in her and the inability to secure good men was the cause no doubt of many perversities to a green crew.

Tapscott's name's being associated with the ship gave food to the chanteyman for his verses and the chantey was seldom sung without the "Good morning, Mr. Tapscott!" It was exceptionally adapted to the heaving up and down of the windlass brakes which, in old ships, worked like an old fashioned fire engine, except that they were never worked from the extreme height to the bottom, in one stroke, but pulled down to the halfway point where it was necessary, on account of the heavy strain from the cable, to change the position of the arms in order to shove the brake to the bottom while the men at the other end were doing the opposite.

Windlass chanties were in 2/4 and 6/8 time, or two beats to the measure, the accent falling nicely as the brakes are pumped, making *Heave Away, My Johnnies* one of the best chanties for this kind of work.

There are several different sets of verses to this chantey but sailor Jack is privileged to use any old words to help out the song.

HEAVE AWAY MY JOHNNIES II

As sung by Fred H. Burgeson, San Francisco

> Oh, heave away, my bully boys,
>   The wind is blowing fair.
> *Heave away my bullies, heave away, oh!*
> Our ship will soon be rolling home
>   To Merry England's shores.
> *Heave away my bullies, for*
> *We're all bound to go.*
>
> Then break her out and square away!
>   We're all bound to go.

Heave Away My Johnnies

Our course lies through those latitudes
    Where stormy winds do blow.

When I was young and in my prime,
    I sailed in the Black Ball line.
They were the finest ships e'er seen
    Upon the ocean brine.

One morning Bridget Donahue
    Came down the dock to see
Old Tapscott 'bout a steerage berth
    And presently said she:

"Good morning, Mr. Tapscott,"
    "Good morning, ma'am," said he.
"And have you got a packet ship
    To carry me o'er the sea?"

"Oh, yes, I've got a packet ship
    To carry you o'er the sea."
"And, please ye, Mr. Tapscott, sir,
    What might the fare then be?"

"It may be fifty pounds," says he,
    "And it may be sixty, too,
But eight pounds ten we'll call enough,
    My pretty dear, for you."

"And here's the money, sir," says she,
    "Step right on board," says he.
"The tide is up, and the wind is fair,
    And soon we'll tow to sea."

"At last!" says Bridget, "I'm off
    To the land so far away,
Where Barney went two years ago,
    The land of Americay."

> Go shake her up my bully boys,
>> This day we're bound to go;
> The anchor is aweigh, and now,
>> For home we'll sing heigh-ho.

Jerry then changed to a pumping chantey, *Clear the Track, Let the Bulgine Run.*" This chantey usually started unblemished and drifted into the obscene. Its being a good song, I'll start it unblemished.

CLEAR THE TRACK, LET THE BULGINE RUN[1]

CAPSTAN AND PUMPS

Moderato

Oh, the wild - est pack-et that you can find, Ah —

he, ah–ho, are you most done? Is the *Mar'-gret Ev-ans* of the

Black X line, So clear the track, let the bul-gine run. To me

high rig - a - gig in a low back car, Ah —

he, ah - ho, are you most done? With E - li - za Lee up —

on my knee. So clear the track, let the bul - gine run.

Clear the Track, Let the Bulgine Run

Oh, the wildest packet that you can find,
    Ah-he, ah-ho, are you most done?
Is the *Mar'gret Evans* of the Black X line,
    So, clear the track, let the bulgine run.

To me high rig-a-gig in a low back car,
    Ah-he, ah-ho, are you most done?
With Eliza Lee upon my knee.
    So clear the track, let the bulgine run.

We screwed the cotton so hard to stow,
In Mobile Bay, with a tale of woe.

Oh, Eliza Lee is the girl for me,
She's the girl I picked up on the quay.

Oh, the wildest packet you can find,
Is Eliza Lee, brailed up behind.

Jerry sang until the cable was short (up and down), when the mate, who watched proceedings from over the bow, sang out, "Avast heaving!" and going to the break of the t'gallant fo'c'sle, raised his hands to his mouth for a speaking trumpet and shouted to the captain, "Anchor's short, sir!"

"Very well, sir!" answered the captain. "Send a couple of men aloft to loose the courses and topsails and heave away your anchor."

"Aye, aye, sir!" answered the mate and in the same breath he ordered,

"Heave away the windlass!" This was answered by the men,

"Heave away the windlass, sir!"

Clank, clank, clank, dropped the pawls, as the windlass revolved; the heaving became harder and harder as the anchor refused to let go and the men gave all their strength as they hove away at the windlass brakes, giving utterances to expressions, "Heave! Oh, Heave and bust her! Heave and let go!" etc., till finally, with the aid of the towboat alongside, the ship forged ahead and the anchor yielded from its clutch below, while the heaving became easier as the anchor was on its way to the surface of the water. Then the mate called again to the captain,

19

"Anchor's aweigh, sir!" while the men kept on heaving the anchor up to the hawsepipe.

The topsails hanging from the yards, we then proceeded to set the sails. The fall of the main topsail halliards was then taken to a snatch block hooked into an eyebolt in the deck for that purpose and with four men at the hoist and the rest of us stringing across the deck, we hauled away to the cry from "Handsome Charlie," with his "Yo-ho! Raise him ahoy!"

Charlie was always dressed well in clean clothes of navy blue. He was always good-natured and a likeable fellow and, on account of his clear complexion and clean face, devoid of whiskers, with pink cheeks, was dubbed "Handsome Charlie." This name stuck to him for the entire voyage.

He started his cry, or sing out, in a low soft tone, but as the work became harder he increased the tone in proportion to the work. This Norwegian had an exceptionally musical sing out and always took the lead in our watch. It is surprising what a difference it makes to the pull. If the chanteyman has a true voice the work is entered into more vigorously. If his voice is not quite up to standard, the men pull in a listless manner.

Stringing across the deck with out feet braced and pulling most energetically, the patent sheave blocks of the topsail halliards kept up a lively accompaniment to "Handsome Charlie's" cry, as the yard was being mastheaded. There is, indeed a merry tone to the click of the ball bearing rollers in the sheave; a feeling that the big blocks above are doing their utmost to help poor Jack lighten his work and one can hear them say, "Go it, old boy! I'm with you!"

With "Handsome Charlie" at the hoist it will not be out of place to give his peculiar sing out in raising the topsail.

HANDSOME CHARLIE'S SING OUT

A - way   hey!   Oh, haul him high - o!

'Way,   hey!   Oh, haul him high- o!

'Way,   hey!   Oh, haul him high-o!

High   -   o!   Raise him and haul him high-o!

'Way hey! Oh, haul him high-o!
'Way hey! Oh, haul him high-o!
'Way hey! Oh, haul him high-o! High-o!
Raise him and haul him high-o!

He kept this up until out of breath, when Jerry came to his rescue by starting *Whiskey*, the chantey I so much wanted to hear. This chantey was generally sung upon getting under way at the topsail halliards and I would certainly have been a disappointed boy had they started some other chantey. Every deepwater sailor knew it as a child knows his ABC's, and while I knew the song I had never sung it pulling on the end of a topsail halliard.

WHISKEY
HALLIARDS

Oh,   whis - key is the   life of   man.   Oh,

whis - key, John - ny! It al - ways was since time be - gan, Oh, whis - key for my John - ny!

Oh, whiskey is the life of man.
Oh, whiskey, Johnny!
It always was since time began,
Oh, whiskey for my Johnny!

A whiskey ship and a whiskey crew,
When whiskey goes then I'll go too.

Oh, whiskey made me wear old clothes,
And whiskey gave me a broken nose.

Oh, whiskey caused me much abuse,
And whiskey put me in the calaboose.

Oh, whiskey killed my poor old dad,
And whiskey drove my mother mad.

Oh. whiskey here and whiskey there,
And whiskey almost everywhere.

If whiskey comes too near my nose,
I tip her up and down she goes.

I drink it hot and I drink it cold,
I drink it new and I drink it old.

Oh, whiskey straight and whiskey strong,
We'll raise the yard to this old song.

Whiskey

Oh, whiskey made the bos'un call,
"Pull all together! One and all."

I think I heard the "Old Man" say,
"We'll splice the main brace here today."

Oh, bring a drink to the chanteyman,
In a glass, or cup, or an old tin can.

Here comes the cook with a whiskey can
And a glass of grog for every man.

A glass of grog for every man,
And a bottle full for the chanteyman.

And so we sang until the mate sung out, "Belay! Belay the main topsail!"

This chantey is one of the best for a drag chantey. The pull comes nicely on the accented notes. With the mastheading of the main upper topsail, we hoisted the fore and mizzen upper topsails and the *Akbar* heeled over nicely.

The bunt gasket of the foresail having been let go, this big sail hung in heavy festoons above our heads only waiting for the clew garnets and buntlines to be released. Here the mate sang out, "Foretack down!" and releasing the weather clew garnet, the port foretack brought the clew of the foresail down to a flat, convex iron hook about three inches wide, through which it rendered while being boarded. The hook was like an elongated "S," the smaller end hooking into a ringbolt on top of the cathead. With a lazy tackle, the rope tack was relieved and a chain, clipped into the clew iron, took its place and was taken to the capstan where it was made fast. When the clew was brought down sufficiently, the mate called, "Make fast the tack!" and the next order was, "Haul aft the foresheet!"

"Haul aft the foresheet, sir!" was answered cheerfully by the men and a couple rushed aft to lend a hand. The sheet was loosely hanging from the lee clew and a lot of slack rope must necessarily come in. If the cook is properly onto his job he will be watching from the galley for the order as our cook did. This is the only rope he is supposed to help with in making sail or tacking ship and if he is not "Johnny on the spot" he is liable to get his curses the same as any old sailor.

Our cook, Brainard, was a middle-aged man and knew his duty, for he shot out of the galley door when the order to "Haul aft the fore-sheet" was given and, throwing the coil from the belaying pin in true sailor style, braced his foot against the spare spar and with his hands close up to the sheave in the rail, flung the loose rope behind him as he pulled hand over hand as fast as he could, entering into the spirit as a fox terrier might shake a rat; and by his runaway yell he brought in the slack as follows:

HAULING IN THE SLACK OF THE FORESHEET

A - way - a - a - ah - hey - a - a - hey. Etc.

Away-a-a-ah-hey-a-a-hey. Etc.

Instead of running along the deck with the rope, which was customary and often done with the braces, the man hauling in the sheet took his position close up to the sheave in the bulwarks, where the rope came through from the outside, and with one foot braced against the spare spar, which rested in a chock on top of the waterways and was lashed to the bulwarks, he could pull and sing out to his heart's content.

Our crew by this time were all feeling the effects of the whiskey they had brought aboard and were in the right mood for anything. With the order to set the main topgallant sail, which is a long hoist, but not as heavy as the topsails, these gypsies of the deep, with muscles of steel, laid hold of the halliards, which are on the opposite side of the ship from the topsails, and in like manner ran their hands up the rope high above their heads, now swaying to the right and again to the left, as they pulled in unison, using their strength of arm as well as their bodies. The merry click of the patent blocks playing an interlude before the sing out soon brought forth the cry, "Oh, masthead her, ahoy!"

The Drunken Sailor

Jerry, who was exceptionally jubilant, having imbibed quite freely from the bottle in the fo'c'sle, and just in the mood for another chantey, started *The Drunken Sailor,* giving all a chance to sing with him. This chantey is usually sung with a solo and chorus, but the condition of the men determines entirely how it shall be sung and there is nothing out of the way if all sing in unison. It was fifty-fifty with us and I doubt if they could have been headed off with a club, so earnest were they in their desire to be heard.

THE DRUNKEN SAILOR (UP SHE RISES)

HAND OVER HAND

up she ris -es ear - ly in the morn - ing.

What shall we do with the drunken sailor?
What shall we do with the drunken sailor?
What shall we do with the drunken sailor?
Early in the morning.

Away, hey, up she rises!
Away, hey, up she rises!
Away, hey, up she rises!
Early in the morning.

Chuck him in the longboat till he gets sober.
Chuck him in the longboat till he gets sober.
Chuck him in the longboat till he gets sober.
Early in the morning.

Away, hey, up she rises!
Away, hey, up she rises!
Away, hey, up she rises!
Early in the morning.

What shall we do with a drunken skipper?
Lock him in his stateroom till he gets sober.

What shall we do with a drunken chief mate?
Put him in the lazaret till he gets sober.

What shall we do with a drunken steward?
Lock him in the galley till he gets sober.

What shall we do with a drunken doctor?
Put him in the coal locker till he gets sober.

What shall we do with a drunken boy?
Hoist him to the royal yard till he gets sober.

John François

The drunken doctor mentioned in this chantey doesn't refer to a doctor of medicine. The cook of the vessel is dubbed "Doctor," but whether the name was given him on account of his mixing qualities, in concocting palatable dishes for the crew from salt beef and briny pork with wormy sea biscuits, or in rationing out lime juice in hot climates as a preventive of yellow fever I am unable to say. Be it as it is, all used the term and it was as natural for a sailor to address him as "Doctor" as it was to call the mate "Mister" or the carpenter "Chips" — a little matter of sailor etiquette understood by the whole crew.

Then at the fore topgallant halliards we followed the custom where all deepwater ships sing the old familiar *John François*.

This old chantey has raised the fore topgallant sail nearly as often as *Whiskey* on the main topsail.

JOHN FRANÇOIS (BONEY WAS A WARRIOR)

HALLIARDS

Boney was a warrior.
  Away-i-oh!
Boney was a warrior,
  John Fran-çi-wah

Boney was a warrior,
A warrior and a tarrier.

Boney fought the Roosh-i-ans.
He licked the Danes and Proosh-i-ans.

He was a soldiers' mutual friend,
And on him France did much depend.

He crossed the Alps, renowned and famed;
He and his brave and glorious men.

He led them on to Moscow.
He led them on to Moscow.

When Moscow was ablazing,
He stood in contemplation.

Then on the plains of Waterloo,
The allied forces he tried to subdue.

But Johnny Bull condemned him.
Yes, Johnny Bull condemned him.

They sent him off to Elba.
They sent him off to Elba.

From there to St. Helena.
From there to St. Helena.

On St. Helena, his body lies low.
France's chance to avenge him, very slow.

They all do pity poor Bonaparte;
He surely died of a broken heart.

Setting the main topsail staysail and taking a turn under the belaying pin, O'Rourke and "Handsome Charlie" began swaying off. The halliards led down to the starboard side of the fife rail around the mainmast. Bracing their feet below and grasping the halliards above their heads these two men swayed away from the bitts, throwing their bodies backward for all the weight they had. This brought the halliards down until their bodies stood at right angles from the fife rail, then bending their knees and holding all they had gained, they rendered the rope under the pin while I pulled in the slack ready for another pull.

A Sing Out

The sing out for this kind of work varies in call from "Yo-ho, he-oh!" or "A-hoy, boys!" with this pull coming on the last word, to a semi-chantey. "Handsome Charlie" broke out in the latter — one of negro origin.

A SING OUT

Oh, Mary! Come down with your bunch of roses! Come down when I call, Oh, Mary! Oh, Mary come down

Oh, Mary! Come down with your bunch of roses!
Come down when I call, Oh, Mary!
Oh, Mary, come down.

Here, the pull for the sway off comes on the accented notes. In the same measure a hold or pause is necessary while the rope is being rendered under the belaying pin, giving time for the men to regain their feet and secure a fresh hold on the halliards above.

Mary and Julia are favorite names aboard ship, with the sailors, particularly in the sway off, and the cry of "Oh-ho, Julia!" denotes a heavy pull all together, on Julia.

When we were about four hundred miles from the Cape of Good Hope the wind increased to a gale and began to blow great guns. All hands were on deck and we clewed up the mainsail to take it in and raced up the rigging, running out on the yard to hand it. Time after time we had the sail almost under control when the gale would blow it from our grasp. The heavy wet canvas was very severe on our hands. Digging away with our fingers' ends against the sail it refused to yield enough to allow us to pinch a seam, with our bleeding nails, for a hold. With the rise of the bow over a sea, during which the wind would spill more or less from the sail, we gradually picked up, inch by inch and foot by foot, the big sail, holding it under our stomachs where we were at a disadvantage, to roll the sail upon the yard. Dave and I were in the quarter of the yard, where he told me to sit on a footrope and see if I could pass the gasket under the yard and over the sail to him for a temporary stop to keep the sail from blowing out again.

Releasing my hold on the sail, I sat down on the footrope, as in a swing, with one arm around the stirrup that supports the footrope from the jackstay, holding the bight of the gasket in my other hand. After several attempts he finally caught the rope and passing it to me, behind the yard below, he pulling up on the gasket above and I pulling down, we held the sail well up against the yard and a couple more turns held it securely.

Then came the task of rolling the sail on top of the yard with the toss of the bunt. All sailors have been well educated in the art of swearing and on the *Akbar* they were all proficient and not backward in blaspheming as they tried, in vain, to raise the heavy, wet sail, cursing the luck that made them sailors, with expressions, "Who wouldn't sell a farm and go to sea!" "Oh, why did I leave my happy home!" etc., all of which was taken good-naturedly in spite of the blue air from the foul mouths with which they damned the ship, the ship carpenters for building her, the captain and officers for sailing her, and themselves for being found aboard her. It made no difference who they cursed. They were there to swear and they certainly did it. Finally, "Handsome Charlie," who was in the slings of the yard, sang out,

"Give her *Paddy Doyle*, Jerry."

This is a chantey for tossing the bunt and is never heard anywhere else. Ships of today have no enormous bunts as a rule, for the clews of the sail are brought up to the yardarms.

Although there is not much music in the chantey it produces results. The words would indicate that Paddy Doyle must have been a fat man who couldn't bend over far enough on account of his belly, to pull on his sea boots. The same was true with us, on the yard, where we were holding with our stomachs, chests and elbows, all the sail we had gathered in and were loath to let go our hands for a fresh hold, farther down, for fear we should lose what we had already gained. But with Jerry starting, "To me way-a-hey," our feet were thrown high in the air, regardless, while our heads went down, with bodies hanging over the yard, as we reached below in another attempt; and with the pause, "O," drawled out, everybody on the yard began the chorus in unison, holding all we had, knowing full well that it required a long pull, a strong pull and a pull all together, as we sang, "Paddy can't dive for his *boots!*"

On the word *boots,* down came our feet under the yard, every man pulling as one, and up rolled the sail, little by little, with the help of the song. Cursing was forgotten and a broad smile broke over the faces of the shellbacks who, a moment before, hated themselves.

This is one of the many places on board ship where the chantey does more to accomplish results than all the swearing, driving, pulling and hauling could otherwise do. A little song does more to lighten the work than the average person can possibly conceive. It changes the disposition of the men like magic. A moment before they were fighting mad; each one puffing and fuming like a spirited animal, working beside a calm dray horse pulling a heavy load out of the mire. If the high-spirited animal would do less jumping and snorting and wait for the word from the driver, when both should pull at the same time, the team would pull the load much easier. We have all seen it ashore, and so with the sailors. There must be teamwork to accomplish any heavy undertaking and the chantey, wherever sung, marks the time where all willing arms must pull in unison.

With several lines of *Paddy Doyle* bordering on the obscene, the words that we sang cannot be given here. Strange to say, all those men knew what was coming for they sang the lines as if they were reading from a book, so familiar were they with the chantey. One seldom hears more than two verses of the song, however, to toss a bunt in a ship of this size.

PADDY DOYLE AND HIS BOOTS

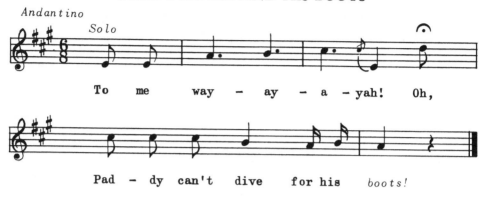

To me way-ay-a-yah!
Oh, Paddy can't dive for his *boots!*

To me way-ay-a-yah!
We'll pay Paddy Doyle for his *boots!*

We'll roll up the sail as we sing, a-yah!
And pay Paddy Doyle for his *boots!*

We'll toss up the bunt with a fling, a-yah!
And hang Paddy Doyle for his *boots!*

We'll all drink whiskey and gin, a-yah!
And hang Paddy Doyle for his *boots!*

To me way-ay-a-yah!
We'll all sling soot at the *cook!*

This little chantey has many changes in the last line of the verse, but it is usually started, as above, with "Paddy can't dive for his boots." And after Paddy's boots have been paid for and he is hung, etc., the chanteyman finds words for the bo'sun and officers, generally ending with the cook, who is looked upon as the scum of the earth.

On reaching Melbourne we came to an anchor off Williamstown, and the next morning the steamer *Resolute* came alongside as we were finishing breakfast and we were called to heave up anchor. Dave, who had been telling me of the different places of amusement in Melbourne, was quite jubilant at the thought of getting ashore, and shipping the windlass brakes, he could hardly wait for the order to "Heave away," before he started the home chantey that he had prepared and taught the other members of the crew the day before. His voice could not be compared to Jerry's, but he was a good chanteyman, outside of a decided nasal twang; he also had the happy faculty of making up rhymes to fit the occasion as he chanteyed, which was immensely enjoyed by all. With the order, "Heave away," he broke out as follows:

SOUTH AUSTRALIA[2]

WINDLASS

South Aus - tra -lia   is my na - tive land. Heave a-way!

Heave a - way!   Moun - tains rich in   quartz and sand. I am

bound for South Aus-tra - lia.   Heave a - way!

Heave a - way!   Heave a-way, you   Rul - er King, I am

bound   for   South Aus - tra - lia.

South Australia is my native land.
    Heave away! Heave away!
Mountains rich in quartz and sand.
    I am bound for South Australia.
Heave away! Heave away! Heave away, you Ruler King,
    I am bound for South Australia.

Gold and wood brings ships to our shore,
And our coal will load many more.

Here's a packet off the pier,
There's a bar ashore with foaming beer.

Heave! Oh heave! And we'll all go ashore.
Where we will drink with girls galore.

Glasses filled we'll touch with a clink,
Heave! Bullies heave! The girls want a drink.

I see Julia standing on the quay,
With a dame for you and me.

At the head of Sandridge Railroad Pier,
Straight to Mother Shilling's we'll steer.

Julia slings the she-oak at the bar
And welcomes sailors from afar.

In the dance hall there you'll pick your girl
With golden hair and teeth of pearl.

She will drink you blind while at the bar,
And call you, "Dear, my own Jack Tar."

She'll waltz you round in a dizzy dance,
While you're half drunk and in a trance.

Then we'll drink to Mother Shilling's name,
And drink again to the lovely dame.

In the arms of girls we'll dance and sing,
For she-oak will be Ruler King.

Drunk! For she-oak's gone to our head,
The girls can put us all to bed.

She-oak is the name of a high-proof keg beer made in southern
Australia. A few drinks is generally sufficient to "put a man under the
table."

Chanteying in the cable, we soon had the mud hook off the bottom,
when we were towed up to Old Pier, Sandridge (now called South Melbourne) and dropped anchor again awaiting a berth at the dock. The
Resolute took the captain ashore immediately after.

The following morning we were engaged with the anchors again,
and hove in the slack of the cable to the chantey *Golden Vanitee,* one
of the oldest of English sea songs.

GOLDEN VANITEE
CAPSTAN

There once was a man who was boast-ing on the quay, "Oh,

I have a ship and a gal – lant ship is she, of

all the ships I know, she is far the best to me, and she's

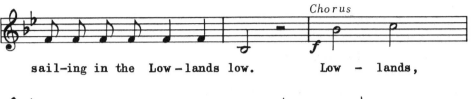

sail-ing in the Low-lands low.   Low - lands,

Low-lands,   she's sail-ing in the Low-lands low.

There once was a man who was boasting on the quay,
 "Oh, I have a ship and a gallant ship is she,
Of all the ships I know, she is far the best to me,
 And she's sailing in the Lowlands low."
Lowlands, Lowlands, she's sailing in the Lowlands low.

For I had her built in the North-a-countree,
 And I had her christened the *Golden Vanitee;*
I armed her, and I manned her, and sent her off to sea
 And she's sailing in the Lowlands low.

Then up spoke a sailor, who'd just returned from sea,
 "Oh, I was aboard of the *Golden Vanitee;*
When she was held in chase by a Spanish privatee,
 And we sank her in the Lowlands low.

"For we had aboard us a little cabin boy,
 Who said, 'What will you give me if that ship I do destroy?'
The skipper said, 'I'll give my child, she is my pride and joy,
 If you sink her in the Lowlands low.'

"The boy took an auger and plunged into the tide,
 And bravely swam until he reached the rascal pirate's side;
He climbed aboard and went below, by none was he espied,
 And he sank her in the Lowlands, low.

"For he took his auger and let the water through,
 And sank the Spanish pirate craft and all her rascal crew;
He swam back to the *Vanitee,* 'twas all that he could do,
 He was sinking in the Lowlands low.

" 'I'll not take you up now,' our cruel captain cried,
    'I'll kill you if you come on deck to claim my child as bride.
I'll throw you in the water, I'll drown you in the tide,
    I will sink you in the Lowlands low.'

"So we took him up, but when on deck he died,
    We lifted him so tenderly, and sewed him in a hide;
We said a short prayer o'er him and dropped him in the tide,
    And he's sailing in the Lowlands low."

The anchor was tripped and the heaving being easier, Jerry gave us a change from the slow chantey to one more cheerful.

CAN'T YOU DANCE THE POLKA
CAPSTAN

As I was strol-ling down the street of bul-ly Lon-don town, I spied a Yank-ee clip-per ship to New York she was bound, and hur-rah! you San-ty, my dear hon-ey, Hur-rah you

New York girls, can't you dance the pol-ka.

As I was walking down the street of bully London Town,
I spied a Yankee clipper ship, to New York she was bound,
And hurrah! You Santy, my dear honey,
Hurrah you New York girls, can't you dance the polka.

She was a neat and little craft, that I met underway;
So I took in all sail and cried, "Way enough, my Rosie May!"

This Yankee lass was clipper built with bluff bow, you must know,
She sailed on land for sailor boys and took them all in tow.

Says she, "You lime-juice sailor, now see me home you may."
But when we reached her cottage door, she unto me did say —

"My flash man, he's a Yankee, with his hair cut short behind.
He wears a tarry jumper and he sails in the Black Ball line."

The *Akbar* sailed from Sydney June 8th, 1876 to Newcastle, for a cargo of coal for Surabaya, Java. The crew shipped by the run and we arrived in Newcastle the following morning. On account of the heavy congestion of ships awaiting cargo, we dropped both anchors in the bay in Hunter River. The runners remained long enough to rig in the jib-boom and unbend the sails.

Awaiting a berth at King's wharf, we remained at anchor until the twenty-eighth, when a gang of men came off to get our anchors up and help dock the ship.

With the variable winds and tide the ship had swung until we counted twelve turns in the cable. These were taken out by putting a seizing around both cables at the water's edge, then the port chain was unshackled at the hawsepipe and the end passed around the starboard chain until the cable was free. The port chain was then reshackled and the seizings cut at the water's edge. Heaving away, our anchors were finally tripped at eight in the evening after a hard afternoon's work.

At nine p.m. we were moored fore-and-aft at King's wharf for our coal. Finished loading coal July 4th, and hauled into the stream letting go the port anchor.

July 7th the new crew came off. All hands sober but one. He was dead drunk and was hoisted out of the runner's boat in a sling that was put under his stomach. Head and feet met below as he was hoisted aboard. His name was Brooks and his home was in Brooklyn, New York. Before the day was over, the crew were all drunk but two.

Brooks awoke about two o'clock crazy with delirium tremens and was locked in the port fo'c'sle. On account of a falling barometer we remained at anchor until July 11th, giving plenty of time for the crew to sober up and put the ship in order.

With the order to "Man the windlass" and "Heave away!" Brooks, having a fine voice, broke out in a chantey called *Santy*.

SANTY

CAPSTAN

Tune: *Can't you dance the Polka*

> As I was lumbering down the street of bully London Town,
> I spied a Yankee clipper ship, to New York she was bound.
> *And hurrah! You Santy, my dear honey,*
> *Hurrah! You Santy, I love you for your money.*
>
> She had the finest clipper rig, now you must understand.
> She did not sail the rolling deep, but cruised upon dry land.
>
> She was a trim old fire ship and rigged out in disguise,
> To burn up sailor boys like me and others damn her eyes.
>
> But when her hawser she stuck out, I made fast to her tow;
> She squared away to a nearby dive and had me on the go.
>
> She filled me full of whiskey, red, and drunk, I fell asleep;
> She rifled all my pockets, boys, and ruined me complete.

While these words pleased the crew, Brooks feeling none too

good from his recent delirium tremens, changed to another chantey, more in keeping with his mood.

SANTA ANA (ON THE PLAINS OF MEXICO)
CAPSTAN

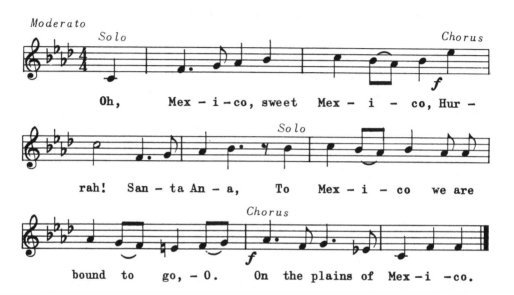

Oh Mexico, sweet Mexico,
    Hurrah! Santa Ana!
To Mexico we are bound to go-o.
    On the plains of Mexico.

Did you ever hear of that General?
Did you ever hear tell of that General?

Oh, Santa Ana rued the day
That ere old Taylor came that way.

He ran away with his old cork leg.
If he hadn't fled he'd have lost his head.

Oh, Santa Ana fought for fame,
And Santa Ana gained his name.

Santa Ana

Oh, Santa Ana's men were brave,
And many found a soldier's grave.

It was a fierce and bitter strife;
Hand-to-hand they fought for life.

Oh, Santa Ana's name is known
For what a man could do was shown.

"Oh, sonny boy, why do you roam?"
"I've got no clothes and I can't go home."

This mournful chanty must have been written, or sung after the close of the Mexican War in 1847. It is indicative of a long, heavy heave at the windlass brakes on a very hot day where the men with tongues hanging out, so to speak, move more or less in a lifeless manner. On days of this kind the chanties in minor keys are resorted to. For as a rule they are sung in slow time. Minor chanties are seldom, if ever, heard in brisk, cold weather.

This was followed up with another ancient chantey:

ONE MORE DAY
CAPSTAN

On - ly one more day, my John - ny,

One more day! Oh, come rock and roll me

o - ver, one more day.

Only one more day, my Johnny,
One more day!
Oh, come rock and roll me over,
One more day.

Can't you hear the Old Man grieving?
Only one more day of heaving.

We can see the Old Man scowling;
Only one more day he's growling.

Don't you hear the windlass pawling?
Only one more day of stalling.

Only one more day of gripping;
Can't you feel the anchors tripping?

Only one more day of working,
And we have no way of shirking.

Heave and pawl! We're never failing.
One more day and then we're sailing.

This is purely an American chantey and was sung at the windlass while heaving up the anchor for the last time. The "one more day" defines itself in that there is to be only one more day spent in the "bloody harbor" and like *Leave her Johnny, Leave her,* the chanteyman sings of petty annoyances of a growly skipper, or mate which he is willing to stand for only one more day. The same rule applies when the ship is wind-bound.

As we tripped our anchor, the towboat *Challenge* took our hawser and with a strong southerly breeze we were soon outside with all sails set.

On the fourth day out we ran into a "southerly buster." Running before it the *Akbar* would settle to port, when a huge sea would come over the rail, filling the decks. The additional weight above would cause her to stagger and tremble all over. With the rise of the wave amidships she would shake like a thing of life trying to clear herself of the weight on deck. The stern settling again, as the sea rushed forward, she righted herself and the heavy mass of water rushed to starboard and away she listed, unable to free herself. The next sea came in over the starboard rail and in like manner we wallowed through each sea, first to port and then to starboard all through the night.

The next day, July 16, the wind backed round to the north and blew great guns. With the ship under fore-topmast staysail, lower fore and main topsails and reefed spanker, we were riding out the gale, which increased in velocity, with a heavy running sea, when we shipped a sea over the starboard bow. It carried away the jib stay and backropes, and stove in the starboard fo'c'sle door and the longboat on top of the fo'c'sle. In this big sea we sprung the bowsprit and foremast. As we were leaking badly, the captain decided to wear ship and head for Sydney.

At the pumps we were wet as drowned rats, trying to avoid the wash by leaving the hand brakes and jumping on top of the main bitts, or anywhere handy with something to hold on to, otherwise our feet would be washed from under and we would find ourselves in the lee scuppers.

In this situation Brooks showed his mettle. While the others were growling and cursing their fate, he shook his head in answer and said, "Well, boys! You are all better off than I and we have all been in this kind of weather before. But when this blows over we'll come about and have fair weather home. We're in for it tonight, but let's forget the weather and try a chantey and heave away cheerily. *Heave Away Cheerily* will be a good one to sing at the pumps." So saying, he led the men in our first chantey since leaving Newcastle.

HEAVE AWAY CHEERILY
CAPSTAN

The wind is free and we're bound for sea.

43

The wind is free and we're bound for sea.
Heave away cheerily ho-oh!
The lasses are waving to you and to me,
As off to the south'ard we go-o,
As off to the south'ard we go.

Sing my lads cheerily, heave my lads cheerily,
Heave away cheerily ho-oh!

Hands at the pumps on the bark *Alice*
(Mystic Seaport 1996.113.1.37L)

For gold that we prize and sunnier skies,
   Away to the south'ard we go.

We want sailors bold who can work for their gold,
And stand a good wetting without catching cold.

The sailor is true to his Sal or his Sue,
As long as he's able to keep them in view.

They're crying, "Come back my dear sailor in blue,
For no one can fill the place vacant by you."

They love us for money, whoever he be,
But when it's all gone, we're shanghaied to sea.

Then sing, "Good-bye Sally, your wonders I'll tell,
But when with another, I'll wish you in hell."

This chantey, although a windlass chantey, was sung at the pumps that evening with words that would hardly look well in print. Brooks knew the crew and sang words for their pleasure, while the seas chased us away from our work from time to time.

Our pumps were of the old hand brake style and, like the windlass, moved up and down, but without a halfway pause. The stroke was directly up and down with a quick motion. Only one pump worked at a time, the one farthest from the handles. Chanteys in 2/4 or 6/8 time can be sung at the pumps where the accent falls on the down or up stroke. During the daytime we seldom started a chantey at the pumps, but during the night we sang one after another during the entire watch.

Brooks was a happy-go-lucky fellow and liked by all. At the pumps his vocabulary in pumping chanteys, which are of the vilest, was at his tongue's end and, knowing this, the sailors begged night after night for a chantey with some spice in it. He generally accommodated them with words from A to Z. This had its effect and pleased the men, for it served to take their minds away from the bad weather and helped them to forget their surroundings.

Hanging Johnny

The next morning had all the earmarks of a pleasant day and the men, while setting the main topsail, were so elated over the prospects of finer weather that Brooks started a chantey when the halliards were thrown from the pin in the rail. We lost no time in hooking the snatch block into the eyebolt in the deck when we tailed on behind and across the deck. No one could help putting his entire strength into the pull of this chantey, for not only were the men's voices unusually good, but the chantey was sung with a jerk and a swing as only chanteys in 6/8 time can be sung. The words were of Negro extraction, yet it was a great favorite with us and sung nearly every time the topsails were hoisted.

HANGING JOHNNY
HALLIARDS

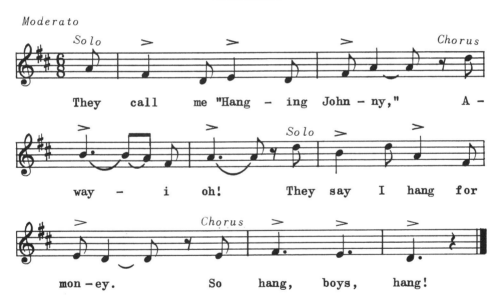

They call me "Hanging Johnny,"
Away-i-oh!
They say I hang for money.
So hang, boys, hang!

Why did you hang your daddy,
And then your mother, laddie?

They say I hung my mother,
And then I hung my brother.

I hung my sister Nancy,
Because I took a fancy.

A rope, a beam, a ladder
I hung them all together.

They call me "Hanging Johnny,"
But I never hung nobody.

I'd hang a brutal mother,
The same as any other.

I'd hang a noted liar
I'd hang a bloated friar.

I'd hang all wrong and folly,
And hang to make things jolly.

Come hang and sway together
And hang for finer weather.

They call me "Hanging Johnny,"
But I never hung nobody.

The words "Hang boys, hang" are used in a topsail halliard hoist, when sweating up the yard "two blocks" where, in swaying off, the whole weight of the body is used. The sing out, from some old shellback, usually words such as "Hang, heavy! Hang, buttocks! Hang, you sons of ----, Hang!"[3]

After setting the topsails we gave her the main topgallant sail, which was all she could carry in a heavy head sea. The decks were awash all day.

With the orders, "Relieve the wheel!" and "That will do the watch!" we took our stations at the pumps as the old stage saying broke out afresh, from those going below, as a parting salute, "Who wouldn't sell a farm and go to sea!" This was too much for the watch on deck and one could hear the curses heaped upon themselves for being caught in a leaky ship like this, etc. But Brooks, in his soothing manner, usually poured oil on the troubled waters and broke out in a chantey — and so we sang and pumped through the watch, interrupted continually by heavy seas coming aboard.

A-ROVING (THE MAID OF AMSTERDAM)
PUMPS OR WINDLASS

Allegretto

Solo

In Am—ster—dam there lived a maid, mark
well what I do say, In Am—ster—dam there
lived a maid and she was mis—tress of her trade, I'll
go no more a-rov-ing with you fair
maid. *Chorus* A-rov-ing, a-rov-ing, since
rov-ing's been my ru-in, I'll go no more a—

rov - ing with you fair maid.

In Amsterdam there lived a maid,
    Mark well what I do say,
In Amsterdam there lived a maid,
    And she was mistress of her trade.
I'll go no more a-roving with you, fair maid.

A-roving, a-roving,
    Since roving's been my ruin,
I'll go no more a-roving with you, fair maid.

Her eyes are like two stars so bright,
Her face is fair, her step is light.

Her cheeks are red, her eyes are brown,
Her hair like glowworms hanging down.

Oh, once I took her for a walk
And listened to her merry talk.

I put my arm around her waist,
Said she, "Young man, you're in great haste."

Said I, "I love you as my life;
How soon will you become my wife?"

I put my hand upon her toe,
And farther then I strove to go.

And then I took her by the heel,
And further still I tried to feel.

I took the lady by the shin,
And further too would I have been.

50

A-Roving

I took the lady by the knee,
And closer still I tried to be.

A-Roving or *The Maid of Amsterdam*, is one of the oldest and
best known chanteys because of its rousing chorus. The words follow
Thomas Heywood's *Rape of Lucrece*, but sailor Jack used words at the
pumps that would put Heywood to shame. Having no ladies aboard,
Brooks availed himself of the opportunity to show his shipmates that
his vocabulary of smutty words was at his tongue's end and he was not
backward in using language not admissible in polite society.

A-ROVING II

Words by Burgeson

In Amsterdam there lived a maid,
   Mark well what I do say,
In Amsterdam there lived a maid,
   And this fair maid my trust betrayed.
I'll go no more a-roving with you, fair maid.

A-roving, a-roving,
   Since roving's been my ruin,
I'll go no more a-roving with you, fair maid.

I asked this maid to take a walk
That we might have some private talk.

And then I took her lily-white hand
In mine as we walked down the strand.

I put my hand around her waist
And snatched a kiss from her lips in haste.

Then a great big Dutchman rammed my bow,
And said, "Young man, dis bin mein vrow."

Then take a warning, boys, from me,
With other men's wives don't get too free.

For if you do you'll surely rue
Your act, and find my words come true.

Brooks distinguished himself by singing the most vulgar words I had ever heard to *The Sailor's Alphabet.* I will not attempt to give them. The words below are sufficient. The definition of each letter that he rendered would hang anyone's head in shame for the remainder of his life. But this seems to have been the custom at the pumps at this time and I cannot use a single letter, as sung by him, to spoil the song.

THE SAILOR'S ALPHABET

A, is for an-chor, you ve-ry well know, and
B, is for bow-sprit shipped o-ver the bow. C, is for cap-stan a-
round which we run, and D, is for der-rick which
hoists in the rum. So Hi-da-ry ho-da-ry
Hi-da-ry dee, No mor-tals on earth are like

The Sailor's Alphabet

sail-ors at sea. Roll a—way, rock a—way, roll us a—long; give

sail – ors   their   grog   and there's   no – thing goes wrong.

A is for anchor, you very well know, and
B is for bowsprit shipped over the bow.
C is for capstan around which we run, and
D is for derrick which hoists in the rum.

So hi-da-ry ho-da-ry hi-da-ry dee,
No mortals on earth are like sailors at sea.
Roll away, rock away, roll us along;
Give sailors that grog and there's nothing goes wrong.

E is for ensign, at our mizzen peak flew, and
F is for fo'c'sle, in which lived the crew.
G is for gangway, where we all do stand, and
H is for hawser, which never will strand.

I is for iron, we hammer all day, and
J is for jib, which we run up the stay.
K is for keelson, which runs fore and aft, and
L is for lanyard, we use on the craft.

M is for mainmast, so good, stout and long, and
N is for needle, that ne'er pointed wrong.
O is for oars, to our jolly boat, and
P is for pennant, so merry did float.

Q is for quadrant, to look at the sky, and
R is for rudder, we steer the ship by.
S is for stun'sle, to help her along, and
T is for topsails, we hoist with a song.

U is for union, which we all adore, and
V is for vane, which we flew at the fore.
W is for wheel, where we spend part our time, and
The other three letters, I can't bring in rhyme.

Brooks then switched off to *The Hog-Eye Man.*

THE HOG-EYE MAN
CAPSTAN AND PUMPS

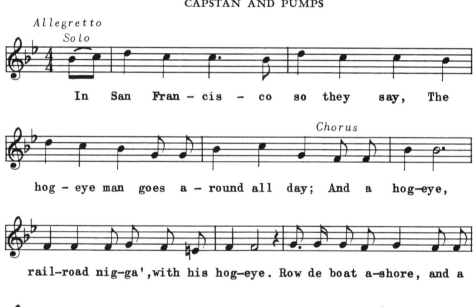

In San Francisco so they say,
The hog-eye man goes around all day;

And a hog-eye, railroad nigga', with his hog-eye.
Row de boat ashore, and a hog-eye.
All she wants is the hog-eye man.

Oh, Sally in the garden, sifting her peas,
Her hair on her head hanging down to her knees.

Oh, Sally looked up and she saw her fate,
For a railroad nigga' came in the front gate.

The hog-eye man gave a fond look of love,
And charmed Sally's heart which was pure as a dove.

Oh, Sally in the garden, sitting on his knee,
She fell for the hog-eye, just in from the sea.

Oh, Sally in the garden, sifting her peas,
She longs for the hog-eye man away to sea.

Oh, "Who's been here since I've been gone?"
A railroad nigga' with his sea boots on.

Oh, Sally in the garden, sifting sand,
She looks for the sailor and the hog-eye man.

In San Francisco, there she'll wait,
For the hog-eye man to walk in the gate.

These words are far more appropriate for the above chantey than those sung by us, for the song is founded on a negro sailor who charmed Sally. She fell for his pleadings and he left her as abruptly as he came into her life. The words of the chantey being of the vilest are not fit to print. Barges in San Francisco during the gold rush were called "hog-eyes". This is where the chantey originated.

Another chantey that he sang was of the same sort. He said it was sung by sailors in the navy, not as a chantey, but as a fo'c'sle song; but we sang it at the pumps as it fitted the time of the pump brakes monotonously working up and down.

CHRISTOPHER COLUMBUS

In four-teen hun-dred nine-ty-two, a   da-go from It -

al-y- o. He's ver-y wise, he's ver-y smart, he sailed the hot ta-

Chorus

mal-e -o. He knew the world was round-o, That

sail-ors all were brown-o, That dirt-y con- ni -ving

son of a gun, was Christ-o-pher Col -um - bo.

In fourteen hundred ninety-two,
    A dago from Italy-o.
He's very wise, he's very smart,
    He sailed the hot tamale-o.

He knew the world was round-o,
    That sailors all were brown-o,
That dirty conniving son of a gun,
    Was Christopher Columbo.

Now, Chris went to the Queen one day
    To ask for ships and cargo.
"In six month's time I'll kiss your hand,
    Or bring you back Chicago."

The Queen she said, "Now look here Chris,
    Your hold is in for trimmin'-o;

Christopher Columbus

You ask for ships, you ask for men,
    But you no ask for women-o.

"Now, sailors must have wives you know,
    Or they will no behave-o."
But Christy say, "That all right, Queen,
    For I've been in the navy-o."

So, one fine day they sail away
    And not a soul was happy-o;
Well, Christy say, "That is all right,
    They're sick in bel', not scrappy-o."

Now Chris had brought his monk aboard.
    The monkey's name was Jumbo,
And all on board they liked that monk,
    Especially Columbo.

The men taught Jumbo how to steal
    Plum duff hid in the galley-o,
So Chris no like the hungry monk,
    Fed Jumbo hot tamale-o.

The monkey stuffed, wouldn't steal by day,
    For duff, he would not bite-o;
So, all hands swore they'd steal that monk,
    But Chris hid monk at night-o.

On one fine night they all got drunk;
    No duff, and sore and grumpy-o,
A sailor said, "Come on me boys;
    We'll all go find the monkey-o."

The monk was found, while poor Chris slept;
    They hazed him till he died-o.
The first mate wept, the second cursed,
    The third mate up and cried-o.

"You finds my monk! You kills my monk!
You abuse my poor Jumbo!
Now I'll find out the whole damn works!"
Said Christopher Columbo.

Then Chris took all the drunken boys
And bound them to the mast-o,
With cat-o-nine tails he did give
Them six and thirty lashes-o.

We had fine weather for a day or two and all sails were set and the decks dried off nicely. At the same time we dried out our mattresses, blankets and clothing which were more or less wet with salt water.

A light breeze springing up from the northward about eight p.m. we were called to make all sail again. The breeze was refreshing, cooling off the air and giving us added life, for we sang a chantey to every sail we hoisted, beginning with *Across the Western Ocean* on the main topsail halliards. This chantey was very popular in the '60s on vessels sailing between London and New York.

ACROSS THE WESTERN OCEAN

HALLIARDS

Heaving the log on the bark *Alice* (Mystic Seaport 1996.113.1.27)

I wish I was in London Town,
   Amelia where're you bound to?
That highway I'd cruise round and round,
   Across the western ocean.

And now we've arrived in London Town,
Our sails are furled and the decks swept down.

The mate's ashore and all the crew
Now what shall we poor sailors do?

We'll do as we have done before;
We'll spend our money and work for more.

We'll spend our money at the Dog and Bell;
If we don't keep sober, we'll all go to hell.

The Rocky Mountains is my home,
Far away from sea and foam.

We then hoisted the fore upper topsail to the chantey, *A Long Time Ago.*

A LONG TIME AGO

LONG DRAG

Capt. J. L. Botterill

A long time a-go I re-mem-ber it well. To me way, hey, hi - o! I had an old wife, oh, I

A Long Time Ago

wished   her   in   Hell.   A   long   time   a - go.

A long time ago I remember it well.
To me way, hey, hi-o!
I had an old wife, oh, I wished her in hell.
A long time ago.

She gave me some money, she gave me some clothes;
And then she turned on me and broke my nose.

My life living with her I could not stand;
So I shipped away for a distant land.

I sold all my clothes, and the money I spent,
And so, off to sea with nothing, I went.

We sailed far away, round Cape Horn,
But I had no clothes to keep me warm.

Our passage we made all safe and sound
And loaded the ship with nitrates, homeward bound.

While off Cape Horn, we had terrible gales;
Our steering gear froze and we lost all our sails.

The next, in the doldrums, six weeks, 'twas a fright.
We boxhauled the packet all day and all night.

We braced and we squared and we tacked and we wore,
And the mate gave us hell worse than ever before.

But soon we will be in Old Dublin again,
And I'll bid good-bye to grief and pain.

And never again from there will I roam,
For the sea is worse than hell at home.

A LONG TIME AGO II

A smart Yankee packet lay out in the bay,
To me way, hey, hi-o!
Awaiting a fair wind to get under way,
A long time ago.

With all her poor sailors all sick and all sore,
For they'd drunk all their lime juice and couldn't get more.

She was waiting for a fair wind to get under way;
If she hasn't had a fair wind, she's still in the bay.

Another set of words by the colored writer, Williams:

A LONG TIME AGO III

Away down south where I was born,
To me way, hey, o-hi-o,
Among the fields of cane and corn,
A long time ago.

I wish now that I'd never been born,
To go cruising round and round Cape Horn.

Around Cape Horn where wild winds blow,
Around Cape Horn through frost and snow.

The wind from the sou-west blowing a gale,
While the packet ship she's crowding on sail.

Oh, Bully John from Baltimore,
I knew you well on the Eastern Shore.

Oh, Bully John was the boy for me,
A bucko on land and a bully at sea.

Oh, Bully John, I knew him well,
But now he's dead and gone to hell.

A Long Time Ago

'Tis a long time and a very long time,
'Tis a very long time since I made this rhyme.

After hoisting the topsails we gave her the fore topgallant sail, sailing in this manner till morning, the main topgallant chain runner's having parted. At eight bells in the morning we slipped a patent link in the broken runner and hoisted the sail to a walk away, *Whiskey*. Quite different from the long drag chantey sung when leaving Boston.

Here we picked up the halliards and tramped across the deck.

WHISKEY II

WALK AWAY

Capt. J. L. Botterill

Oh, there was an Irish barber
    And he came from Aberdeen.
Whiskey, Johnny.
And he had as nice a barbershop

As you have ever seen.
Whiskey for my Johnny.

And there was a rich young lady
    And she dressed herself with care.
And she sent for the barber
    For to comb and brush her hair.

And to make himself look handsome,
    He put on his Sunday clothes,
With his shiny top hat tilted
    O'er his red, red nose.

On his way he met a friend of his
    And to him he did say,—
And they were still drinking whiskey
    Till night relieved the day.

Now this rich young lady waited
    Till the tears began to flow,
For no one could tell her where
    The barber he did go.

Now, early in the morning
    When the barber he did wake,
His clothes were torn and muddy
    And he thought his head would break.

Then he thought of this young lady
    And her hair he had to comb,
And he said, "I'll go and see her,"
    So he started for her home.

And to her house he wandered
    Till he brought up at her door,
And he pushed the door wide open
    And fell sprawling on the floor.

Now this rich young lady ran to him,
    It was her only bet,
So she put both arms around him
    And their lips in kisses met.

"Belay! Belay the main t'gan'sle!" shouted the mate; and so the reader is cut off from the rest of song, which he must finish in imagination.

Another *Whiskey* walk away to the same tune follows:

WHISKEY III
WALK AWAY

I, on Friday went to market
    For a Paddy's dish of meat,
Whiskey, Johnny.
But the fish was old and rotten
    And 'twas scarcely fit to eat.
Whiskey for my Johnny.

So I strolled along the docks
    For a better place to go,
When a fisherman came in,
    Rowing hard as he could row.

"Oh, my good fisherman,
    Have you any fish to sell?
"Yes, mister, here's a crab
    That will suit you very well."

So I took the bugger home
    And for want of plate or dish,
I put him in the pot,
    And he swam like any fish.

In the middle of the night my wife
    Got up to see the crab,

And of course the bugger snapped her,
　　For he had a nifty grab.

"Oh, husband dear, come quick,
　　For my flesh is badly torn!
The devil's in the pot, and
　　He's whacking up his horn!

"Oh, the devil's in the pot
　　And he's whacking up his horn,
And the like I've never heard since
　　The day that I was born."

So, out of bed I scrambled,
　　For I knew it was the crab,
But he caught me by the hand
　　With the other claw he had.

Then my wife she seized a poker,
　　For I then let out a roar,
And between us both we had him
　　Lying dead upon the floor.

Another chantey for light sails:

BLOW BOYS BLOW
HALLIARDS

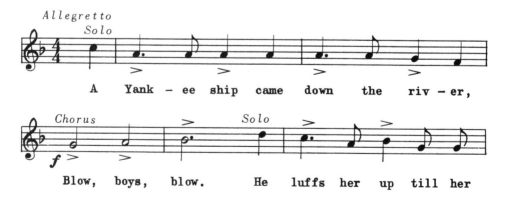

A Yank-ee ship came down the riv-er,

Blow, boys, blow. He luffs her up till her

Blow Boys Blow

top-sails qui-ver, Blow my bul-ly boys, blow.

A Yankee ship came down the river,
Blow, boys, blow.
He luffs her up till her topsails quiver,
Blow my bully boys, blow.

Now, how do you know she's a Yankee liner?
The Stars and Stripes float out behind her.

Now, who do you think is mate aboard her?
Why, Bully Jones is mate aboard her.

He'll ride you down like you ride the spanker.
You'll brighten brass till you see your shadow.

And who do you think is second mate of her?
Some ugly cuss that hates a sailor.

Oh, blow today and blow tomorrow.
We'll blow away all care and sorrow.

And who do you think was steward of her?
Chin Chaw Chinaman from Hong Kong, China.

Oh, what do you think we had for dinner?
Oh, monkeys' lights and donkeys' liver.

And what do you think she had for cargo?
Molasses and monkeys stowed bung up, oh!

As we had thirty days of succeeding gales and calms, I'll give some of the chanteys we sang during this time.

The fore upper topsail was hoisted to the chantey:

POOR OLD MAN

HALLIARDS

A poor old man came riding by.
And I say so, and I hope so,
A poor old man came riding by,
Oh, poor old man.

A poor old man came riding by,
Said I, "Old man, your horse will die."

And if he dies, I will tan his hide,
But if he lives, again I'll ride.

And if he dies, I'll not get the blues,
I'll have his hide to make my shoes.

We'll haul him aft, no questions ask,
And dump him into the harness cask.

Oh, now poor horse your time has come.
Oh, many's the race I know you've won.

Poor Old Man

A derby once you tried to win,
And I was the bloke to carry you in.

Oh, poor old horse you're going to die.
We're going now to say good-bye.

Oh, he has gone and will go no more.
Good-bye old horse for ever more.

THE DEAD HORSE

Tune: *Poor Old Man*

For one long month I rode him hard
And I say so, and I hope so,
And shivered with cold up on the yard.
Oh, poor old horse.

And when he dies I'll tan his hide,
And throw him into the swelling tide.

Sailors receive one month's advance wages before sailing on a long voyage. As the money is usually spent before leaving port, they work the first month for nothing. This is called "working up the dead horse." Old time custom was actually to bury the horse.

A writer who took part in one of these ceremonies says, "The sailors secured some old grain sacks which were in the forepeak, cut out the figure of a horse and sewed the parts together. Each man gave a bit of straw from his mattress and this, with some old trash, they stuffed into the gunny sack horse. During the 6 to 8 dog watch they brought forth the beast. Some kicked and others scrambled to get a hit at him. The horse was hauled upon the forecastlehead and the trial and funeral service began. 'Frisco,' the life of the crowd, standing in front of the horse with a book in his hand, finished his remarks with, 'So, you must die.' He struck the stuffed horse on the head with a serving mallet and began the burial service. After this we carried the horse to the lee cathead and roared out the chantey, *Oh, Poor Old Man your horse will die;* after the chantey the horse was thrown overboard."[4]

One morning Brooks started a whistling chantey at the pumps and jokingly remarked, "It's a good thing I'm not superstitious or I'm afraid I'd never sing this chantey again. We are sure having our share of wind." This song did more to keep the crew good-natured than anything else.

While *Hanging Johnny* had its melancholy tune, the new chantey, *A fal-de-lal-day* was decidedly humorous. The word "fal-de-lal-day" fitting in at the most opportune time usually kept us laughing because it was so ridiculously funny that when it was time for the first chorus, which was whistled by all, not half of the men could pucker sufficiently to whistle—breaking up the song with loud bursts of laughter.

It is not fitting here to give all the words sung by Brooks. Suffice it to say the words in a way followed Thomas Heywood's noted *Rape of Lucrece*. Some of the words are given in *A-roving*, another pumping chantey and by far the most musical of any. It was often sung at the windlass while heaving up anchor.

As we were continually pumping we repeated each line of the following, to make the chantey last longer.

A FAL-DE-LAL-DAY

PUMPS

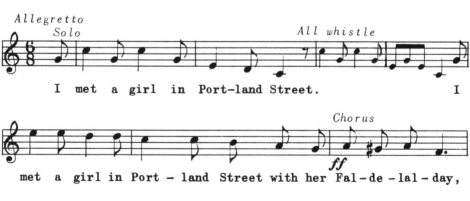

I met a girl in Port-land Street. I

met a girl in Port - land Street with her Fal-de-lal-day,

fal-de-lal-day, fal-de-lal-lal-de-lal-de-lal-day.

A *Fal-De-Lal-Day*

I met a girl in Portland Street.
    (*All Whistle*)
I met a girl in Portland Street *with her*
Fal-de-lal-day, fal-de-lal-day.
Fal-de-lal-lal-de-lal-de-lal-day.
The sweetest girl I chanced to meet.
    (*All whistle*)
The sweetest girl I chanced to meet *with her*
Fal-de-lal-day, fal-de-lal-day,
Fal-de-lal-lal-de-lal-de-lal-day.

Said I, "Young miss, how do you do?"
Said she, "The worse for meeting you."

"Young miss," said I, "I like your style."
Said she, "Young man, just wait awhile."

I took her hand and on we trod;
Said she, "Young man, you're rather odd."

And to her room not far away,
She bade me call another day.

I put my arms around her waist;
Said she, "Young man, you show good taste."

I pulled her down upon my lap.
Said she, "You now deserve a slap."

Her ankle next, I placed my hand;
Said she, "For this I will not stand."

I pulled her dress above her knee;
Said she, "Young man, please let me be."

And why did I no further go?
Alas! Her leg was cork, you know.

With the gale abating and the sea going down, there was the well known cry of "Eight bells! Call the watch and set the main topsail!" It wasn't long before the watch appeared. The snatch block took the halliards and Brooks led in *Riding on a Donkey*.

RIDING ON A DONKEY

HALLIARDS

Capt. J. L. Botterill

Soon we'll be in London Town.
Sing ye lads, hi-oh!
We'll see the queen with a crown.
Sing ye lads, hi-oh!

Riding on a Donkey

Hi-oh! and away we'll go,
Riding on a donkey.

We'll see the girls with eyes of brown
And drink the best there is in town.

We'll clew up sail and heave her to
And never sail till the pay day's due.

At Oxford Circus we'll take our stand
Among the lords and ladies grand.

My gal I'll dress in ribbons bright
And at Garrie's show we'll spend the night.

We'll drink the best he's got in store,
And when it's gone we'll call for more.

The fore topsail was set to our pet chantey, *Hanging Johnny*. No singing on the poop for the mizzen topsail, we hoisted the main top-gallant sail to *Tommy's Gone to Hilo*.

TOMMY'S GONE TO HILO
HAND OVER HAND

Oh, Tom-my's gone, what shall I do? a-way-y, Hi-lo-o. Tom-my's gone and I'll go too. Tom-my's gone to Hi-lo.

Oh, Tommy's gone, what shall I do?
Away-y, Hilo-o.
Tommy's gone and I'll go too.
Tommy's gone to Hilo.

To Hilo town, we'll see her through,
For Tommy's gone with a ruling crew.

Oh, Tommy's gone from down below,
And up aloft this yard must go.

Oh, Tommy's gone, we'll ne'er say nay
Until the mate sings out, "Belay!"

I think I heard the old man say
We'll get our grog three times a day.

Oh, one more pull and that will do,
So let her roll and wet us through.

We did not keep our good weather very long, for the next day the wind sprang up from the southwest with a heavy cross sea, and again Friday was our hoodoo.

The watch was called to shorten sail and I held the wheel until all was secure above. After being relieved and going down the lee poop steps I found the men at the main bitts taking in the slack of the topsail sheet to a sing out I had never heard before, which ran as follows:

SHORT DRAG

Corn broom, hick-o-ry broom, squil gee swab!
Corn broom, hickory broom, squill gee swab!

Swaying off on the pull the others came out strong on the word *swab*. The pull was a strong one and had as its result, besides giving a little sunshine, a smile drawn forth by the old set, "Yo-ho boys"—and it left the men in better spirits. They needed some variety, for in such weather we were all more or less tired out, grouchy and ill at ease.

After snugging her down we again started the pumps, when Brooks broke out in *A fal-de-lal-day* and "Dublin" tried to shut him off saying, "For God's sake, Brooks, lay off that chantey and give it a rest. I'm not superstitious, but damn it to hell, try somethin' else." Brooks only laughed and kept on with the song, but when it came to the whistling chorus he and I were about the only ones to whistle.

Brooks was not a man to irritate anyone and it didn't take long for him to see that the men were dissatisfied and troubled, so he wound up the chantey in quick order, switching to *Clear the Track, Let the Bulgine Run,* in which he used words only befitting a pumping chantey.

The gale blowing strong from the north the ship was hove to almost continually from July 28th to July 31st when it moderated and we set the reefed foresail and reefed mainsail. While rousing home the main sheet, the second mate led the men in *Haul Away, Joe.* There was not much music in his voice, but how he could pull when chanteying! He seemed to have the strength of three men and the watch doubled their efforts to keep up with him. Mr. Sanborn was similar to Brooks in his vulgarity, but he put more life into the men and heavy work seemed easy when he condescended to jump in and lend a helping hand.

The men were strung out along the deck, knee-deep in water, where they held the sheet of the sail, and the second mate took his position close up to the sheave, standing on top of the spare spar, one hand free and swinging in the breeze he sang at the top of his voice so as to be heard above the gale by us all. There was a merry twinkle in his eyes that I will never forget as he looked over the shoulders of the men awaiting the last word, "Joe!" They all knew the song and knew what to expect.

Few people can understand what it means to sing in such weather. It was absolutely necessary to stretch the foot of the sail all it would stand, to bring the clew as far down as possible. Having no steam it was up to us to do the work—which could not be done on this ship without the short drag chantey. Here, the second mate, singing at the top of his voice as he neared the end, suddenly turned, grasping the sheet with both hands while he crouched with bended knees, and on the word "Joe!" straightened out with one mighty pull. With the help of the others it brought the rope whizzing through the sheave, while I held the turn around the pin and took in the slack as the men rendered it up to the pin.

HAUL AWAY, JOE
SHORT DRAG FOR FORE AND MAIN SHEET

Saint Patrick was an Irishman, He came from Dublin City.
He drove the snakes from Ireland, and then drank all the whiskey.
A-way, haul a-way, haul a-way, Joe!

Saint Patrick was an Irishman,
    He came from Dublin City.
Away, haul away, haul away, Joe!
He drove the snakes from Ireland,
    And then drank all the whiskey.
Away, haul away, haul away, Joe!

He built a church in Limerick,
    And on it he put a steeple.
He held high mass for forty days,
    But couldn't fool the people.

Away, haul away,
    Come haul away my Rosie.
Away, haul away.
    My Rosie she's a posy.

Setting the fore royal on the bark *Alice* (Mystic Seaport 1996.113.1.12)

Oh, once I loved an Irish girl,
  But she was small and sassy,
And once I loved a French girl,
  Oh, say, but she was naughty.

Oh, once in my life I married a wife,
  And, damn her, she was lazy,
And wouldn't stay at home of nights
  Which damn near set me crazy.

She stayed out all night, Oh hell! what a sight,
  And where do you think I found her?
Behind the pump, the story goes,
  With forty men around her.

I have often thought how easy it would be for a crew of deepwater sailors to enter a tug of war contest, with every man's son, flat on his back and with feet braced with the stretch of the rope pulling his utmost, then a nice little chantey like *Haul Away, Joe* would completely upend the men on the opposite side and bring home the bacon.

With the call of the watch at eight bells we came about and stood on the starboard tack, hoisting the upper main topsail to a walk away chantey. The sun was shining brightly and the spirits of the men revived when going aft to set the mizzen upper topsail. We had never sung a chantey on the poop knowing that the captain despised a chantey, but he had just "shot the sun" and was below figuring up our position, so Brooks gave us the wink and he started—

STORM ALONG JOHN
HALLIARDS

Oh, Storm A-long John was a son of a gun, to me

Storm Along John

way – hey – a Mis – ter Storm A–long. Storm – y's gone and

Chorus

I 'll go too. To me way, Oh, Storm A–long.

Oh, Storm Along John was a son of a gun,
To me way-hey-a Mister Storm Along.
Stormy's gone and I'll go too.
To me way, oh, Storm Along.

Stormy, he is dead and gone.
A good old man was Storm Along John.

They dug his grave with a silver spade;
His shroud of the finest silk was made.

They lowered him down with a golden chain,
Their eyes were dim with more than rain.

He was a sailor bold and true;
A good old skipper to his crew.

He lies low in an earthen bed,
Our hearts are sore, our eyes are red.

He's moored at last and furled his sail
No danger now from wreck and gale.

Old Stormy's heard an angel call,
So sing his dirge now, one and all.

There are several "Storms" with slightly different airs which I give
here. Sailors had a way of twisting the words to suit their mood.

STORM ALONG JOHN II

HALLIARDS, HAND OVER HAND

Old Stormy he is dead and gone,
To me way-a, Storm Along.
Old Stormy he is dead and gone,
Oh, come along, get along, Storm Along John.

Old Stormy he was a bully old man.
Old Stormy died and we dug his grave.

Storm Along John was a good old man,
He served his sailors grog by the can.

He gave us plenty of spud hash, too,
And every Sunday we had Black Ball stew.

He never put us on our whack,
No pound and pint, "according to The Act."

Then shake her up and away we'll go,
We're bound to sail, blow high or low.

Storm Along John

I wish I was with Storm Along
A-drinking of his rum so strong.

For Storm Along was a good old rip
As good a man as ever sailed a ship.

STORM ALONG JOHN III

HALLIARDS

Oh, Storm - y was a son of a gun. To me

way, hey Storm A-long John. Oh, Storm-y he was a

son of a gun, High-aye-aye Mis-ter Storm A - long.

Oh, Stormy was a son of a gun.
To me way, hey, Storm Along John.
Oh, Stormy he was a son of a gun,
High-aye-aye Mister Storm Along.

STORMY

HAND OVER HAND, HALLIARDS

Old Storm - y he was a bul - ly old man. To me

way, you Storm A-long. Old Storm-y he was a
bul-ly old man, Aye, aye, aye, Mis-ter Storm A-long.

Old Stormy he was a bully old man.
To me way, you Storm Along.
Old Stormy he was a bully old man,
Aye, aye, aye, Mister Storm Along.

Old Stormy's dead and gone to rest;
Of all the sailors he was best.

For fifty years he sailed the seas,
In winter storms and summer breeze.

And now old Stormy's day is done.
We marked the place where he has gone.

He slipped his cable off the Horn,
Far from the place where he was born.

I wish I was Old Stormy's son,
I'd build a ship of a thousand ton.

I'd load her with New England rum,
And all my shellbacks they'd have some.

Storm Along John was very popular on all merchantmen, but the
'Badian negroes took great delight in singing the words in many varia-
tions and when once started would sing one after another, changing the
air to suit their mood.

Stormy

A merry twinkle in the eyes of the chanteymen and a smile from the others joining in on the chorus, told better than words how much it was appreciated.

STORMY II

HALLIARDS, HAND OVER HAND

Oh, O Stormy O, Stormy he was a son of a gun,
  To me way-oh, Storm Along John.
Oh, Stormy he was a son of a gun,
  Way-oh, Storm Along John.

OLD STORMY

HAND OVER HAND

Storm A-long John. *Solo* Old Storm-y he is dead and gone, Ah- *Chorus*

ha! Come a - long, get a - long, Storm A - long John.

Old Stormy he is dead and gone.
To me way, hey, Storm Along John.
Old Stormy he is dead and gone,
Ah-ha! Come along, get along, Storm Along John.

POOR OLD JOE

HALLIARDS, HAND OVER HAND

Marcato
Solo
Old Joe is dead and gone to Hell, Oh, we *Chorus*

say so, and we hope so, *Solo* Old Joe is dead and

Chorus gone to Hell. Oh, poor old Joe.

Old Joe is dead and gone to hell.
Oh, we say so, and we hope so,

Poor Old Joe

Old Joe is dead and gone to hell.
Oh, poor old Joe.

The ship did roll, the winds did roar,
He's dead as a nail on the lamp room floor.

He won't be hazing us no more.
We hope to God his sins are o'er.

Poor old Joe is one of the oldest chanteys, and was sung in both English and American ships.

SUN DOWN BELOW
HALLIARDS

Words by Masefield

Six o'-clock, I hear 'em say, Sun down – Sun down be-low.

Aye – a   a – a – a – – Sun down – sun down be-low.

Six o'clock I hear 'em say,
Sun down, sun down below.
Aye-a a-a-a
Sun down, sun down below.

De day's been hot, yo' all do say,
Time to quit and go away.

Pack our duds and dinna' pail,
Come back sure befo' you sail.

Sun Down Below, Mobile Bay, Way Sing Sally and *Hilo, My Ranzo Way,* are purely West Indian negro chanteys sung while hoisting cargo from the hold of ships and seldom if ever sung by sailors at the halliards.

MOBILE BAY

HAND OVER HAND

Were you ebba in Mobile Bay?
John, come tell us as we h'ist away.
A-screwin' cotton all de day,
John, come tell us as we h'ist away.
Aye, aye, h'ist away.
John, come tell us as we h'ist away.

Badian nigga' h'ists at de fall;
Just got back from de ol' Black Ball.

Bends his back, shows white ob his eye;
Works too hard an' it makes him sigh.

Sweat rolls down in de middle ob his back;
Stinks like a nigga' on de railroad track.

Don't yo' heah dat ol' dingdong?
Time to quit. Eight bells done gone.

WAY SING SALLY
HAND OVER HAND

'Badian coon chantey

Sally am de gal just like a daisy.
　　Way, sing Sally.
She turns me around till I'm half crazy.
　　Sally am de gal fo' me.

Sally she's a 'Badian bright mulatto;
She nebba' uses snuff or chews tobacca.

Sally am de gal dat lubs dis nigga';
Now stay away black man, yo' cuts no figga'.

Sally dressed up in her new suit ob clo's;
See all de nigga's look around where ebba she goes.

Nigga' in de corn fiel' actin' up bold,
Oh, Sally hit de nigga' an' knocks him out cold.

It is h'ist an' sing while de mate is naggin';
He growls all de day wid his dingin' an' a-dangin'.

Nebba min' de weather, but keep yo' legs togedda;
De fair land ob Canaan will soon be a-showin'.

HILO, MY RANZO WAY

HAND OVER HAND

I'm Ran-zo Jim from de South-ern cot-ton grow-ing belt, To me

way, hey - oh, hi, oh! De sun am so hot dat you'd

think a man would melt, And sing, Hi - lo, my Ran-zo way.

I'm Ranzo Jim from de southern cotton growing belt,
To me way, hey-oh, hi, oh!
De sun am so hot dat you'd think a man would melt,
And sing, Hilo, my Ranzo way.

We picked all de cotton an' threw it in de basket,
An' de boss said 'twas g'wine far up de Naragasket.

So I came right along into old Mobile Bay,
Where de nigga's all work in de cool ob de day.

A-screwin' cotton in de big ship's hol',
"Dat's all I'd have to do," so I was tol'.

De work was so hard dat I near done broke my back;
So dis nigga' wants a job befo' he gets de sack.

So I'd like to sail on a little pleasure trip,
Where de work ain't so hard, on a Yankee sailing ship.

Den de mate said to me, "Come as soon as you are able.
All you've got to do is to scrape de rusty cable."

Another set of words runs:

O, the boys and the girls went a huckleberry hunting;
O, the girls began to cry, and the boys they stop'd hunting.

Then a little girl ran off, and a boy he scampered after,
And the little girl fell down and he saw her little garter.

He said, "I'll be your beau if you'll have me for a feller,"
And the little girl said, "No! For my sweetheart's Johnny Miller."

Ranzo is purely a Southern negro term used in the cotton ships at Mobile and New Orleans, and also sung by the 'Badian negros at the fall.

Brooks ventured to sing another chantey, *Reuben Ranzo,* which is one of the oldest and is purely a hoisting chantey. It was used as a long drag for the topsails and also as a hand over hand hoist for lighter sails, where the pull comes twice as quick.

Reuben Ranzo was depicted as a joskin; a man that was not very bright. Such sailors the officers called "joskins" or gave them the name of "Reuben." When a man was once called Reuben the crew were not slow in following up, and the name stuck throughout the voyage.

REUBEN RANZO[5]
HALLIARDS

Do you know old Reu-ben Ran-zo? Ran-zo, boys, oh,

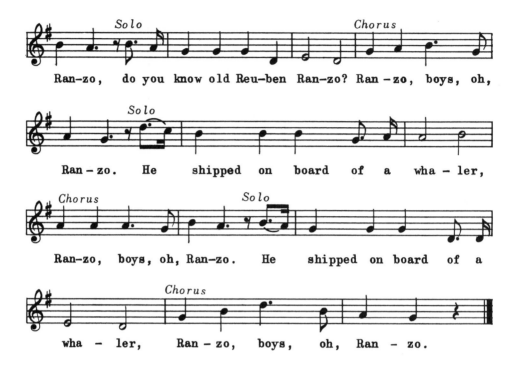

Ran-zo, do you know old Reu-ben Ran-zo? Ran-zo, boys, oh, Ran-zo. He shipped on board of a wha-ler, Ran-zo, boys, oh, Ran-zo. He shipped on board of a wha-ler, Ran-zo, boys, oh, Ran-zo.

Do you know old Reuben Ranzo?
Ranzo, boys, oh, Ranzo.
Do you know old Reuben Ranzo?
Ranzo, boys, oh, Ranzo.
He shipped on board of a whaler,
Ranzo, boys, oh, Ranzo.
He shipped on board of a whaler,
Ranzo, boys, oh, Ranzo.

Oh, Ranzo was no sailor;
For Ranzo was a tailor.

Oh, Ranzo joined the *Beauty*,
But he could not do his duty.

The *Beauty* was a whaler,
And Ranzo was no sailor.

Reuben Ranzo

The mate he being a hard man,
He was just like old sailors ran.

He took him to the gangway
And said, "I'll cut your two hundredth lay."

He took him to the grating,
Where Reuben was then shaking.

This act was surely dirty,
For he gave him six and thirty.

And then he quit and let him go.
And I pity you, Reuben Ranzo.

But the captain being a good man,
He down the steps to Reuben ran.

He took him to his cabin.
He took him to his cabin.

And gave him wine and brandy,
For which he grew quite handy.

He raised him in his station,
And taught him navigation.

He married the captain's daughter,
And sailed across the water.

Oh, Ranzo was a tailor,
But now he is a sailor.

And now he's Captain Ranzo.
Hurrah! For Captain Ranzo.

After setting the topsails, we sang *Blow the Man Down* at the top-gallant halliards. This chantey is one of the oldest and best known of all, a great favorite in all ships; and on account of the jingling rhyme it is easy for the chanteyman to make up words at the hoist. It has been sung so often that the words are legion.

BLOW THE MAN DOWN
HALLIARDS

Blow the man down bullies, blow the man down,
And away, hey, blow the man down.
Blow him right down from the top of his crown,
Give me some time to blow the man down.

As I was walking down Paradise Street,
A saucy young damsel I chanced for to meet.

She backed her main topsail and gave me a sigh,
And said she was busted and ready to die.

Blow the Man Down

"Oh, Jack," said the maiden, "And will you stand treat?"
"Oh-i, me dear lady, let's walk down the street."

She steered me through alleys and up to the bar,
And had me quite groggy before going too far.

She told of a clipper just ready for sea,
And said she was waiting for sailors like me.

This fine full-rigged clipper, to Sydney was bound.
She told how well manned, and so very well found.

She slipped me her hawser and took me in tow,
And soon I was anchored in Battery Row.

And, so I was shanghaied aboard this old ship;
She took all my money and gave the slip.

As soon as the clipper was clear of the bar,
The mate knocked me down with the end of a spar.

'Tis larboard and starboard — away we all sprawl,
For our bo'sun's Jack Rogers, the worst of them all.

When the captain he stands at the break of the poop,
You'll jump, or he'll hit you a belt in the snoot.

I'll give you a warning before we belay,
Don't ever take heed of what pretty girls say.

*   *   *   *   *

There was an old sailor, in London did dwell;
He had a young wife, but he wished her in hell.

His wife became sick, acting strangely and bad,
For all that she craved was a big deep-sea crab.

This chantey was usually sung by white sailors, ending the chorus
on the key note. But the negroes in Barbados sang it, employing their

93

harmonious functions by ending the chorus strong on the fourth above, which was very effective and pleasing to the ear.

BLOW THE MAN DOWN II

Come listen to me and a story's my aim,
And away, hey, blow the man down.
It's of an adventure I met with a dame,
Give me some time to blow the man down.

While cruising around, and out for a spree,
I met a flash packet, the wind blowing free.

What country she hailed from, I couldn't tell which,
But from her appearance she looked like a witch.

Her flag was three colors, her mastheads were low,
She was round in the counter and bluff in the bow.

I fired my bow chaser, the signal she knew;
She backed her main topsail and quickly hove to.

I spoke her in English, her tongue very loose,—
"I'm from the 'Blue Anchor', bound for Paddy's 'Gray Goose'."

"What is your cargo, my sweet pretty maid?"
"I'm sailing in ballast, kind sir," she said.

"I'm as neat a young skipper as ever was seen."
"I'm just fit for a cargo; my hold is swept clean."

I gave her my hawser. She took me in tow,
And yardarm to yardarm, down street we did go.

We jogged on together, so jolly and gay,
Till we came to an anchor in Ratcliffe Highway.

Then, hoisting our topsails and away we both bore,
For a sailor's snug harbor, for a berth and to moor.

She brailed in her spanker, her stuns'ls and all,
I rigged in my jib boom and gun tackle fall.

I've fought with the "Rooshians", the "Prooshians" also,
I've fought with the Yankees and Johnny Crapeau;

But of all the strange dames that I ever did see,
She beat all the stinkpots of heathen Chinee.

The topsails having been set, the ship once more heeled over in her accustomed manner, and by dropping and hauling aft the sheet of the foresail she carried about as much sail as she wanted. Here Brooks broke out in another old-timer when the sail refused to flatten with our combined effort. All hands available strung forward, along the deck, with feet braced and arms extended, our calloused hands gripping the foresheet awaiting the final word of the chorus, in which all hands give one sudden strong pull while singing, "Haul the Bowline, the Bowline, Haul!"

This chantey, like *Haul away, Joe,* is sung by the chanteyman without a pull from anyone until the final word of the chorus, *"Haul!"* Then, everyone pulls his mightiest and the clew of the sails comes down foot by foot, until the mate sings out, "Belay! That'll do the foresheet!"

HAUL THE BOWLINE

SHORT DRAG

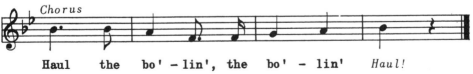

Haul the bowline,
Kitty is my darling.

Haul the bowline, the bowline haul!
Haul the bowline,
    The bully mate is snarling.
Haul the bowline, the bowline haul!

The albatros' are soaring,
So early in the morning.

The packet ship's a-rolling,
The skipper is a-growling.

She's making heavy weather,
We'll buckle off together.

We'll give her hell and blazes,
And fiddlestring her braces.

We'll either break or bend her,
We're all wet through, God damn her.

The spray flew over the house as she bumped into the head sea, and we again got a taste of what we thought we were rid of. Not satisfied with the foresail, our next order was "Set the mainsail!" Gaskets were thrown off and we attempted to board the maintack while the big sail thrashed and flapped above our heads.

If one has ever seen a silk salesman unroll a bolt of silk and double it over in his fingers, giving it a sudden jerk, snapping it to show its texture, let him fancy a sheet of No. B cotton duck overhead with ropes and blocks beating against the sail as the wind whipped the folds of canvas athwartships. Flapping and snapping in rapid succession, not rolling thunder. The captain, with speaking trumpet in hand, would be giving orders to the mates. They shouted themselves hoarse in answer, ordering the men to all parts of the ship at once, because the mainsail refused to yield to the pull and haul of the men who were trying their best to bring the weather clew down to the hook in the stanchion of the bulwarks.

There is not much melody in the following, but results were obtained from chanties of all sorts, and I think we sang during this spell of

weather all the known chanties of the day. We roused home the tack
to the tune of:

JOHNNY BOKER

SHORT DRAG, TACKS AND SHEETS

Andantino
Solo

Do my John—ny Bo—ker, come rock and roll me

Chorus

o—ver. Do my John—ny Bo—ker, Do!

Do my Johnny Boker,
    Come rock and roll me over.
Do my Johnny Boker, Do!
Do my Johnny Boker,
    From Calais town to Dover.
Do my Johnny Boker, Do!

A steady gale is blowing,
The Yankee ship is rolling.

Come pull and haul together,
We'll either bend or break her.

The Old Man he's a-growling
The gale is now a-howling.

The weather's thick and hazy,
The mate is damn near crazy.

Our arms are sore and aching,
Our hearts are near to breaking.

Oh, haul and sway together,
Come haul for finer weather.

Come haul and drown our sorrow,
'Twill all be gone tomorrow.

All hands hauling on the word, *Do!* of this short drag chantey our work was soon accomplished and we were sent to leeward to "haul aft the main sheet!"

Here Brooks gave us a change from a good old rousing chantey to a sort of chant with obscene words, where the pull again comes in on the last word.

SLAPANDER-GOSHEKA

SHORT DRAG, TACKS AND SHEETS

poo, slap–e–ter, slap – an – der–go– she – ka, slap–*poo!*

What would my mother say to me,
    If I should come home with Big Billy?
Slap-poo, slap-e-ter,
    Slap-an-der-go-she-ka, slap-poo!

I'd tell her to go and hold her tongue,
For she did the same when she was young.

Oh, have you got lady, a daughter so fine,
That's fit for a sailor who's just crossed the line?

I'm tanned from the tropics and sailed from afar,
My jacket is greasy and covered with tar.

I smell of bilge water pumped out in Hong Kong,
But give us your flipper and help me along.

Your daughter, I've heard is some dame on the street;
I've come for to ask, what's the chances to meet?

This chantey, if it could be called one, is not often heard, but it served to give us a little variety, and from that time on we hardly picked up a rope without singing some kind of a chantey.

The last gale went down as quickly as it had sprung up, and the ship rolled heavily, slatting the sails against the mast all through the night. The next day, August 3rd, the steamer *Challenge*, our old friend, took our hawser and at 12:30 a.m. we sighted Sydney Heads light. At 2:30 a.m. the pilot came aboard and seeing our condition remarked that if there ever was a "lame duck" entering port, the *Akbar* certainly had a right to that name.

After breakfast the first thing was to pump her out. The brakes were shipped and for the last chantey we pumped her out to:

LEAVE HER JOHNNY, LEAVE HER
PUMPS

Oh, pump her out from down be - low, Oh, leave her John - ny, leave her. Oh, pump her out and a - way we'll go, For it's

time   for   us   to   leave   her.

Oh, pump her out from down below,
  Oh, leave her, Johnny, leave her.
Oh, pump her out, and away we'll go,
  For it's time for us to leave her.

Oh, the times are hard and the ship is old,
And the water's six feet in her hold.

The starboard pump is like the crew,
It's all worn out and will not do.

They made us pump all night and day,
And we half dead had naught to say.

The winds were foul, the sea was high;
We shipped them all and none went by.

She'd neither steer, nor stay or wear,
And so us sailors learned to swear.

We swore by note for want of more,
But now we're through we'll go ashore.

We'll pump her out, our best we'll try,
But we can never suck her dry.

The rats have gone and we, the crew,
It's time by God, that we went too.

The *Akbar*, after unloading her coal into an old hulk, went into
Fitzroy drydock, on Cockatoo Island, where the copper was stripped
from her bottom and she was recalked and recoppered.

Returning to the hulk for our coal, the foremast, bowsprit, and
mizzen topmast being sprung, and the rudder-head twisted, they were

replaced by new ones. Everything was taken off the ship except the main yard. As our standing rigging was of hemp, the riggers agreed to rerig the ship in wire giving $500.00 to boot for the hemp rigging, which was accepted. We remained in Sydney until November 14th, when we hove up anchor to the chantey *The Cruise of the Dreadnaught*, bound again for Surabaya, Java.

CRUISE OF THE DREADNAUGHT
CAPSTAN

It is of a flash pack—et, and a pack—et of fame. She is

bound to New York and the *Dread-naught's* her name. She's

bound to the west—ward where strong winds do blow; She's a

Liv —er—pool Lin—er, bul—ly boys let her go. Bound a—

way, bound a—way, where strong winds do blow, Bound a—

way in the *Dread-naught* to the west—ward we'll go.

It is of a flash packet, and a packet of fame.
　　She is bound to New York and the *Dreadnaught*'s her name.
She's bound to the westward where strong winds do blow;
　　She's a Liverpool Liner, bully boys let her go.

Bound away, bound away, where strong winds do blow,
　　Bound away in the Dreadnaught *to the westward we'll go.*

And now we are hauling out of Waterloo dock,
　　Where the boys and the girls on the pierhead do flock;
They give us three cheers while their tears freshly flow,
　　Bound away in the *Dreadnaught* to the westward we'll go.

And now we are laying in the Mersey all day,
　　Waiting for the *Constitution* to tow us away.
All around the Black Rock where the Mersey does flow;
　　Bound away in the *Dreadnaught* to the westward we'll go.

And now we are sailing on the wild Irish Sea,
　　And the passengers below, they are drinking so free,
While the sailors like larks up aloft to and fro,
　　Bound away in the *Dreadnaught* to the westward we'll go.

And now we are crossing the oceans so wide,
　　Where the dark and blue billows dash against our black side.
With sails spread so neatly the red cross will show,
　　Bound away in the *Dreadnaught* to the westward we'll go.

And now we are crossing the banks of Newfoundland,
　　Where the water is green and the bottom is sand.
The fish in the ocean swim around to and fro,
　　Bound away in the *Dreadnaught* to the westward we'll go.

Oh, the *Dreadnaught* she's flying past Old Nantucket Head;
　　And the man in the chains takes a cast of the lead.
When up scoots a flounder just fresh from the ground,
　　Crying, "Blast your eyes, chucklehead, mind where you sound."

And now we are sailing down Long Island shore,
    Where the pilot boards us, as he's oft done before.
"Fill away your main topsail! Board your main tack also!"
    She's a Liverpool packet, Lord God, let her go.

And now we are anchored in New York once more;
    "Here's health to the *Dreadnaught,* she's the ship brought us o'er."
You may talk of your packets *Swallowtail* and *Black Ball,*
    But the *Dreadnaught*'s a clipper, and she beats them all.

There are a number of verses to the above song, as it was very popular in early days and each chanteyman had words of his own.

The *Constitution* was a company tow boat, and the Red Cross, the company's emblem, was a large Greek cross, as used in the flag of Great Britain. It reached from the foot of the fore topsail to the close-reef band.

In the 1880's there was probably no ship so much talked of as the *Dreadnaught.* She was built in Newburyport, Mass., in 1853 by Currier and Townsend, and was 1413 tons register; length 210 feet; breadth 40 feet; depth 26 feet, a semi-clipper. She was able to bear driving as long as her sails and spars would stand. She was owned by Governor E. D. Norman, Francis B. Cutting, David Ogden and others who subscribed to build her for Captain Samuel Samuels. He superintended her construction and sailed her in David Ogden's "Red Cross Line", with the *Victory, Racer,* and *Highflyer.*

Captain Samuels was a man to hang on, under royals, passing other vessels under reefed topsails. Under such conditions, sailors called her "The Wild Boat of the Atlantic," "The Phantom Ship," "Flying Dutchman," and other names.

She was considered by many to have made the fastest passage from New York to Queenstown, having the reputation of sailing the run in February 1859, in the remarkably short time of 9 days and 17 hours.[*]

On account of losing a rudder in a heavy head sea and the ship's refusing to head up by use of drags, Captain Samuels had the distinction of sailing the *Dreadnaught* stern first, 183 miles in 52 hours, before a jury-rudder could be made and shipped. This feat is no doubt unprecedented. The hurricane disabled the *Dreadnaught* in what is termed by the Atlantic sailors, "The Devil's Blue Hole." The center of it is about Lat. 45° N, Long. 45° W; about 360 miles from Fayal, which port he finally reached in safety.

The *Black Ball Line* is another famous chantey we sang. Not many writers give the original words, for the chanteyman, as a rule, used the words to *Blow the Man Down*.

THE BLACK BALL LINE

CAPSTAN

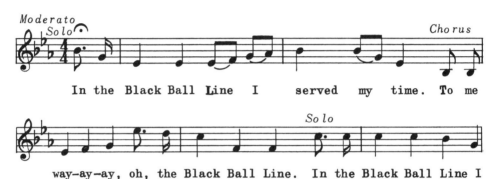

In the Black Ball Line I served my time. To me way-ay-ay, oh, the Black Ball Line. In the Black Ball Line I

served my time. Hur-rah for the Black Ball Line.

In the Black Ball Line I served my time.
To me way-ay-ay, Oh the Black Ball Line.
In the Black Ball Line I served my time.
Hurrah for the Black Ball Line.

Our dead horse we'll work ('tis a month's advance pay.)
So heave away bullies and get under way.

Our anchor we'll cat at the fish tackle fall,
And sing a good chorus on this old Black Ball.

We'll sing to the girls we have left on the shore,
But Liverpool town will supply plenty more.

Oh the doctor cooks for one and all;
But what do we get on this old Black Ball?

Soup and bully, lob scouse, dandy funk and duff,
Weevil bread, sour spuds, and salt horse that is tough.

Then sheet home the topsails; sing high derry dee
Haul aft the fore sheet, for we're now bound to sea.

We jump and we swear, for the mate is boiled hard;
Look out for a marlinspike dropped from the yard.

We'll rattle her down and the shakin's we'll save,
For the Old Man's as tight as a corpse in the grave.

In the above song, soup and bully (soup and bouilli) is beef boiled with vegetables, lob scouse is a meat stew, dandy funk is a sweet pudding or dumpling seasoned with molasses, and duff is pudding cooked with raisins or dried apples.

A negro writer named Williams wrote the following words sung to this chantey. A number of his chanties were published in a monthly magazine about the year 1920. This chantey was sung at least a hundred years ago. In the old Black Ball Line days they knew nothing of the Civil War words furnished by Williams. His words belong to *Blow the Man Down*.

THE BLACK BALL LINE II

Come all you Black Ballers and listen to me,
    To me way-ay-ay, Oh the Black Ball Line.
Come along, come along and I'll sing you a song.
    Hurrah for the Black Ball Line.

In the Black Ball Line I served my time;
In the Black Ball Line it's rise and shine.

Shanghaied by McCormack aboard a Black Ball,
With tinkers and tailors, shoemakers and all.

I then joined the navy and became a Yank,
But they put me aboard of an old iron tank.

The *Monitor,* she is the latest craft,
Just like a cheesebox stuck on a raft.

Old Erickson was the identical man
Who first invented the catamaran.

The *Monitor* fought the *Merrimac,*
And sent her home with a broken back.

The pioneer Black Ball Line ships came out in the year 1816, sailing from New York to Liverpool. They carried a large painted black ball below the close reef band in front of the fore topsail.

JOHNNY GET YOUR OATCAKE DONE (JAMBOREE)

CAPSTAN

And now, my boys, be of good cheer, for the

I-rish coast is draw-ing near. In a few days more we'll

sight Cape Clear. So John-ny get your oat-cake done. Oh,

Jam-bo-ree, oh, jam-bo-ree, oh go a-way black man,

don't-cher come a-nigh me. Jam-bo-ree, oh,

jam - bo - ree, oh, John -ny get your oat -cake done.

And now, my boys, be of good cheer,
  For the Irish coast is drawing near.
In a few more days we'll sight Cape Clear,
  So, Johnny get your oatcake done.

Oh, Jamboree, oh jamboree,
  Oh, go away black man, don't-cher come a-nigh me.
Jamboree, oh jamboree,
  Oh, Johnny get your oatcake done.

This chantey was a great favorite in the 60's, across the Western Ocean, when the record passages were made by the *Dreadnaught* and the *Andrew Jackson* of the North American Line, Black Ball Line, Swallowtail and Tapscott's Lines. The chanteyman in those days generally took his seat on the capstan head in chanteying, while warping into the dock, for there was always a crowd on the pierhead to hear the chanteying and it was the skipper's pride to dock under these conditions.

The above words were given me by Captain Nye. When I was a boy I used to sing it using the words, "Johnny get your hoe-cake done."

Another set of words that were used to the air of *Johnny get your Oatcake Done* was a chantey called *Early in the Morning*, when bound for London.

EARLY IN THE MORNING

Now my boys to home we're near,
  The Lizard Light is burning clear,
The Lizard Light is burning clear,
  So early in the morning.

Now my boys we're at Gravesend,
  We're nearly at our journey's end;
We're nearly at our journey's end,
  So early in the morning.

Now my boys we're in the docks,
The pretty girls come out in flocks,
The pretty girls come out in flocks,
So early in the morning.

On account of the lateness of the year, when light winds and calms abound in Torres Straits and about New Guinea and other islands inhabited by cannibals and pirates, the captain considered it unwise to attempt going through the Straits and took the southern route, south of Tasmania and up the west coast of Australia.

Not much happened of interest, outside of the regular routine aboard ship, except that we had our usual run of gales off the southern coast and while the *Akbar* was a much better sea vessel than when leaving Newcastle, recalked, recoppered and reloaded, she still shipped plenty of water. While on the starboard tack we made three or four inches per hour; "Rig the pumps" was not a strange sound. On the port tack she was not so bad. "Leaking just enough to keep her sweet," said the captain.

We reached Surabaya, Java, on January 21st, 1877, and began unloading our coal with the help of nine coolies who worked on deck. We shoveled the coal into small bamboo baskets which were passed by hand to the coolies above who in turn dumped the coal into a barge alongside.

After all the coal was out except about one hundred tons left for stiffening, the between-decks and sides were swept clean for our new cargo of sugar which came off in lighters or scows holding from 100 to 200 baskets. They were large cylindrical baskets, or mats, about five feet long and weighing from 500 to 700 pounds. As we had no donkey engines a purchase was rigged from the main yardarm to handle the sugar. The fall, leading through a snatch block in the deck, was taken to the main deck capstan where an awning was spread to keep off the sun. The pawls of the capstan were triced up and the capstan bars lashed in. The end of the fall was stopped around the barrel of the capstan so we wouldn't lose it in letting go. Then, walking around the capstan, we hove the sugar up above the rail where a tackle from the main stay was hooked into the sling and when "high" and ordered to "let go," we stepped aside, letting go of the capstan bars which whizzed round as the fall unwound without restraint, while the sugar swung

108

over the main hatch, snubbed by the second mate who held the turn at the rail and lowered it into the hold where it was stowed away by the coolies.

To break up the monotonous work of walking around the capstan all day we sang many a chantey to lighten the work. Our first one was started by Archie. It was the *Banks of Sacramento*, an old California packet ship chantey in the 50's.

BANKS OF SACRAMENTO

Oh, New York's race course is nine miles long. To me hoo-dah! To me, hoo-dah! Oh, New York's race course is nine miles long, To me, hoo - dah! Hoo - dah - day! Then it's blow my bul - ly boys, blow, for Cal - i - for - ni - a. There's plen -ty of gold so I've been told, on the banks of Sac -ra -men -to.

Oh, New York's race course is nine miles long,
  To me, hoo-dah! To me, hoo-dah!
Oh, New York's race course is nine miles long,
  To me, hoo-dah! Hoo-dah-day!

Then it's blow my bully boys, blow,
  For Cal-i-for-ni-a.
There's plenty of gold so I've been told,
  On the banks of Sacramento.

A bully ship and a bully crew,
A bully mate and a skipper too.

Oh, New York's race track where we stood,
We bet on all they said was good.

Our watch, our shoes, and every rag,
But lost our money on a bobtail nag.

Our money all gone we shipped to go,
Around Cape Horn where strong winds blow.

We're bound for Cal-i-for-ni-o!
For gold and banks of Sacramento.

This chantey was evidently taken from Stephen Foster's *De Camp-town Ladies.*

In order to make the chantey last throughout the hoist the chantyman usually repeated each line of the verse. It had a rousing chorus in which every man opened his mouth, singing his utmost. The song rolled across the water in the still air and was echoed back from a large Dutch ship off the starboard beam which had her sails dropped for drying from the rain of the night before.

We had noticed a couple of ladies on the ship who shifted their chairs under the awning, evidently for a better position to hear the music. This gave new life to our men and we did our best to please them selecting chanties with a rousing chorus where we all could be heard.

Rio Grande

"Give 'em *Rio Grande* or *Shenandoah*," said Williams.

"*Rio Grande*," we all clamored and Archie began the chantey using words from an old Mother Goose rhyme and branching off to words of the windlass chantey as given below.

RIO GRANDE

CAPSTAN

"Oh, where are you go-ing to, my pret-ty maid?" A-

way, oh, Ri-o! "Oh, I'm go-ing a-milk-ing,

sir," she said, For we're bound for the Ri-o Grande. Oh, a-

way, oh, Ri-o! A-way, oh, Ri-o! So fare you well, my

bon-ny young girl, For we're bound for the Ri-o Grande.

"Oh, where are you going to, my pretty maid?"
Away, oh, Rio!
"Oh, I'm going a-milking sir," she said.
For we're bound for the Rio Grande.

111

Oh, away, oh, Rio!
Away, oh, Rio!
So fare you well, my bonny young girl,
For we're bound for the Rio Grande.

"Oh, may I go with you my sweet pretty maid?"
"I'm sure you're quite welcome, sir," she said.

Oh, man the good capstan and run it around.
We'll heave in the sugar and then, homeward bound.

We'll sing to the maidens, come sing as we heave;
You know at this parting how sadly we grieve.

Sing good-bye to Sally and good-bye to Sue,
And you who are listening, good-bye to you.

So heave up the sugar until it is high,
"Let go! Stand from under!" the mate, he doth cry.

Oh heave with a will and heave steady and strong.
We'll sing a good chorus for 'tis a good song.

The ship she went sailing out over the bar,
They pointed her nose for the old Southern Star.

So good-bye, young ladies, we'll sing you no more,
But we'll drink to your health when we all go ashore.

Running around the slack for the next basket we took the strain
and Archie started *Shenandoah,* one of the most musical chanties of all.

SHENANDOAH
CAPSTAN

Oh, Shen-an-doah, I long to see you. Hur –

Shenandoah

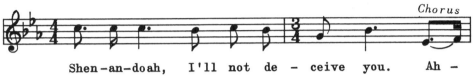

Oh, Shenandoah, I long to see you.
> *Hurrah, you rolling river.*
Oh, Shenandoah, I'll not deceive you.
> *Ah-hah, we're bound away,*
'Cross the wide Mis-sou-ri.

Oh, Shenandoah, I love your daughter,
I love the place across the water.

The ship sails free, the wind is blowing,
The braces taut, the sheets a-flowing.

Oh, Shenandoah, I'll leave you never,
Till the day I die, I'll love you ever.

The topsails hoisted with a song,
She feels the strain and bowls along.

"Masthead that yard!" the mate will say,
"Give one more pull and then, belay!"

Missouri, she's a mighty river.
We'll brace her up till her topsails shiver.

Missouri, she's a mighty river,
The redskins' camp lies on the border.

The white man loved the Indian maiden,
With notions his canoe was laden.

The chief refused the trader's dollar,
"My daughter, you shall never follow."

At last there came a Yankee skipper,
He winked his eye and tipped his flipper.

He sold the chief some firewater,
And 'cross the river he stole his daughter.

The coolies, not to be outdone, and helping at the capstan, surprised us by singing one of their chanteys that was very good indeed. As near as we could gather from the words, it was going from Surabaya to Pasoeroean. It was sung in their language and I will not vouch for the correctness of the words.

FROM SURABAYA TO PASOEROEAN
CAPSTAN

Javanese Chantey

Sum go coolie ah-e-ah ang,
    Sor Surabaya, hoo-e-la-e-la-e-la.
Hoo-e-la-e-la-e-la. Hoo-e-la,
    Sum go Surabaya, sor Pasoeroean.

114

Tailing on the fore topgallant halyard on the bark *Alice*   (Mystic Seaport 1996.113.1.20)

Another coolie chantey that was sung in the hold while stowing the sugar in place was *Ah-hoo-e-la-e*. Four or five coolies to a basket sat on the deck with their feet against the upper part of the basket, and bracing themselves from behind with their hands on the deck, shoved the sugar with their feet in time to the accented notes of the chantey. In cutting or slewing the basket all hands sing in unison with a mighty shove on *"Ung!"* comparable to "Haul Away, *Joe!*"

Ah-hoo-e-la-e was sung from morning till night. All hands and the cook knew it before the ship was loaded.

AH-HOO-E-LA-E
ROLLING SUGAR

Javanese Chantey

Ah, hoo-e la-e, hoo-e-la-e,
Ah-e, hoo-e ah, hoo-e, la-e ung!

An excellent chantey for light work is *Ten Thousand Miles Away*, because of the long solo by the chanteyman. In heavy work, he would be winded should he attempt to sing it.

TEN THOUSAND MILES AWAY
CAPSTAN

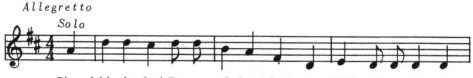

116

Ten Thousand Miles Away

breeze. A bul – ly craft and a cap–tain true to

car–ry me o–ver the seas; To car–ry me o–ver the

seas, my boys, to my true love far a – way; for she's

tak–ing a trip in a gov–ern–ment ship, Ten thou–sand miles a –

Chorus

way. Then blow ye winds high–o, A rov–ing I will

go. I'll stay no more on Eng–land's shore so let the mu – sic

play. I'm off on the morn–ing train to

cross the rag – ing main. For I'm on the move to my

own true love Ten thou—sand miles a — way.

Sing hi! Sing ho! For a gallant bark,
    A stiff and rattling breeze,
A bully craft and a captain true,
    To carry me over the seas.
To carry me over the seas, my boys,
    To my true love far away;
For she's taking a trip on a government ship,
    Ten thousand miles away.

Then blow ye winds high-o,
    A roving I will go.
I'll stay no more on England's shore,
    So let the music play.
I'm off on the morning train
    To cross the raging main,
For I'm on the move to my own true love,
    Ten thousand miles away.

My true love she is beautiful,
    My true love she is young.
With eyes so blue of violet hue,
    And silvery is her tongue.
And silvery is her tongue, my boys,
    And while I sing this lay,
She is doing the grand in a far off land,
    Ten thousand miles away.

Oh, sad and bitter was the day
    When I parted from my Peg;
She'd a government brand upon each hand,
    And another around each leg.
And another around each leg, my boys,

As the ship sailed away,
"Adieu," said she, "Remember me,
Ten thousand miles away."

Oh, the sun may shine through a Dublin fog,
And the Liffey run quite clear,
Or a p'liceman when wanted may be found,
Or I may forget my beer.
Or I may forget my beer, my boys,
Or the landlord's quarter day,
But I can't forget my own true love,
Ten thousand miles away.

On March 16th, we took in our last three lighters of sugar and received the news that we were bound for New York for orders.

March 19th, the captain came aboard in the morning very much excited and immediately gave orders, "Heave up your anchors and get under way!" It developed that he was unable to get three hundred tons of tea and spices. With both anchors down, the ship turning with the tide had a dozen or more turns in the cables. Jim Dunn and I were over the bow taking out the turns, one by one. The mate watching proceedings from above, sang out, "There are seventeen turns below. Dip your end around seventeen times and shackle up again. You work like a mess of coolies!" We did as directed. The seizing was cut at the water's edge and the cable slipped down in tangled mess. With the order to, "Man the windlass!" the port chain came up fouled. The thermometer registered 115 degrees, and as the work became harder Archie started the chantey that was always sung on all deepwater ships leaving a foreign port bound for home.

HOMEWARD BOUND (GOOD-BYE FARE YOU WELL)
CAPSTAN

We're go-ing a - way to leave you now.

119

We're going away to leave you now,
Good-by, fare you well. Good-bye, fare you well.
We're going away to leave you now.
Hurrah, my boys, we're homeward bound.
Then give me the girl with the bonny brown curl.

Homeward Bound

Good-bye, fare you well. Good-bye, fare you well.
Your hair of nut brown is the talk of the town,
  Then, hurrah, my boys, we're homeward bound.

We're homeward bound, I heard them say,
  We're homeward bound with nine month's pay.
Our anchor we'll weigh and our sails we will set,
  The friends we are leaving we leave with regret.

Oh, fare you well, we're homeward bound,
  We'll heave away till our anchor is found.
So, fare you well my Rosy Nell,
  Oh, fare you well, for I wish you well.

Oh, Rosy Nell, I'm under your spell,
  And when far away, I'll wish you well.
Your lips cherry red and your hair to your waist,
  Will long be remembered, though leaving in haste.

Then fill up your glasses for those who were kind,
  And drink to the girls we are leaving behind.
So, good-bye to Sally and good-bye to Sue,
  And those who are listening, good-bye to you.

We're homeward bound across the sea,
  We're homeward bound with sugar and tea.
We're homeward bound and the wind's blowing fair,
  There'll be many true friends to greet us there.

Then, good-bye Surabaya, our anchor's aweigh,
  We'll sheet home the topsails before it's "Belay!"
We'll brace her up sharp and we'll board our main tack,
  'Twill be a long time before we get back.

This chantey is sometimes sung at the windlass, using only the first half, but a good chanteyman can greatly improve the song, which is a rouser with good voices, by singing the double stanza as given above. Williams and Archie were both good chanteymen, never lacking in

121

words, and seldom repeated a line — a thing usually done by inferior chanteymen.

Homeward Bound was followed by *Sally Brown*.

SALLY BROWN (ROLL AND GO)

CAPSTAN

Oh, Sally Brown is a bright mulatto.
  Wa-ay, roll and go.
Oh, she drinks rum and chews tobacco,
  I'll spend my money on Sally Brown.

Oh, Sally Brown is a parson's daughter;
She drinks Scotch without any water.

Sally Brown is a Creole lady,
Oh, she's all right, but a bit shady.

Seven long years I courted Sally,
And seven long years she would not marry.

Oh, Sally Brown why did you leave me?
Oh, Sally Brown, I love none but thee.

Oh, seven long years I loved this lady,
But now she's got a negro baby.

This rousing chantey[7] is one of the best at the capstan where the men watching for the short solo to end, break out strong in the first chorus, "Way-ay, *Roll* and *go*" and buckle down to a heave that fairly bends the capstan bars as the high notes are reached.

The cables coming in foul we switched to an old pumping chantey, *Fire Down Below.* This chantey depicts trouble in different localities about the ship; although a pumping chantey it is often sung at the windlass. The words are senseless, but Sailor Jack is permitted to use any words that bring results — and we sang the following:

FIRE DOWN BELOW
PUMPS

Oh, fire in the topsail yard,
Fire down below.
Oh, fire in the topsail yard,
Fire down below-o-o-o,
Oh-i-o, oh, fire down below,
Oh, oh-i-o, oh, fire down below.

Fire in the windlass, boys,
Fire down below, etc.

Fire in the anchor chain,
Fire in each bower, boys.

Fire in the lower hold,
Fire in between-decks, boys.

Fire in the crossjack yard,
Fire in t'gallant yard.

Each of the above lines was repeated by the chanteyman, who had the privilege of carrying the fire to any part of the ship to spin out the song.

There was another *Fire Down Below* I learned on the *Akbar*, which was purely English. We never sang it, but the 'Badian negroes sang it at the fall. I picked up a set of words from Williams, a negro writer, which I give below[8].

FIRE DOWN BELOW II
PUMPS

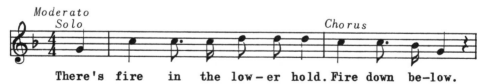

There's fire in the low-er hold. Fire down be-low.

Fire in the main well, and the cap-tain did-n't know.

Fire Down Below

Chorus

Fire, fire, fire down be-low.

Get a buck-et of wa-ter. Fire down be-low.

There's fire in the lower hold.
 Fire down below.
Fire in the main well,
 And the captain didn't know.

Fire, fire, fire down below.
 Get a bucket of water,
Fire down below.

There's fire in the mizzen top,
 Fire down below.
There's fire in the chain plates
 And the bo'sun didn't know.

There's fire in the forepeak,
 Fire down below.
There's fire in the galley
 And the cook he didn't know.

There's fire in the booby hatch,
 Fire in the main,
There's fire in the windlass,
 And fire in the chain.

There's fire in the whole ship,
 The mate he being drunk,

The captain, he just went below
And found him in his bunk.

Shallow Brown was also sung at the fall by the 'Badian negroes.

SHALLOW BROWN
PUMPS OR HOISTING

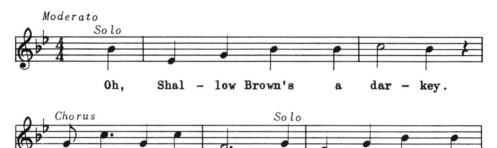

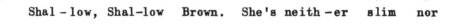

Oh, Shallow Brown's a darkey,
Shallow, Shallow Brown.
She's neither slim nor stocky.
Shallow, Shallow Brown.

Oh, Shallow Brown of New York,
Her feet and legs just like a stork.

Oh, Shallow Brown of Baltimoah,
She's best li'l dancer on de floah.

Oh, Shallow Brown of Washington,
She's got us niggers on the run.

Oh, Shallow Brown of Mobile Bay,
She's picking cotton all de day.

126

Shallow Brown

Oh, Shallow Brown of New Orleans,
She's blackest gal ob all de queens.

Oh, Shallow Brown of Phila-me-delf,
She jumped in de ribba an' drown herself.

As the heaving became harder, we followed *Fire Down Below* with *Lowlands,* giving us a chance to breathe more freely.

LOWLANDS[9]

CAPSTAN

Oh, were you ever in Mobile Bay?
  Lowlands, lowlands, away my John.
A-screwing cotton all the day,
  My dollar and a half a day.

A black man's pay is a dollar a day;
A dollar and a half is a white man's pay.

127

Oh, were you ever in New Orleans?
That's where you meet the Southern Queens.

I wish I was in Slomes Hall,
A-drinking luck to the old Black Ball.

Oh, my old mother, she said to me,
"Come home my boy and quit the sea."

I dreamed a dream the other night,
I saw my love dressed all in white.

She stood and gazed in one blank stare,
And combed the ringlets of her hair.

Her face was pale and white as snow;
She spoke to me in accents low.

"I'll cut away my bonny hair,
No other man shall think me fair.

"I'll cut my breasts until they bleed,
From you, my love, I'll soon be freed.

"I'll jump into the Lowland Sea,
And drown myself for love of thee.

"With seaweed green about my head,
You'll find me there, but I'll be dead."

I then awoke to hear the cry,
"Hey, you sleepers! Watch ahoy!"

The landsman, no doubt sees nothing in the music of this mournful chantey but a mess of doggerel. Having never taken part in the work he cannot understand it. But to the sailor who, at the hand brakes or capstan bars, has spent a half day under a tropical sun, sweating blood, as it were, heaving in a foul anchor that refuses to budge from the bottom, there is a recollection of bygone days that stirs his heart to over-flowing. And should the strains of this old chantey once again fall upon his ears (which is, indeed, unlikely) he no doubt would move heaven and earth for a chance to grasp a handspike or capstan bar, heave his utmost, and help swell the chorus, dragging out the words as of yore, "Lowlands, Lowlands, A-way my John," and then tell of the circumstances under which he sang it on his last ship.

Having no luck with the starboard chain we tried the port. The heaving was much lighter at the start but the farther we got the worse it came in. By the time we finished with *Lowlands,* both anchors dragged together and refused to yield from the bottom. It took all hands at the brakes, on one side, to heave her down and the strain was so great that the windlass brakes were badly bent and had to be straightened with a top maul. Then we lashed a boom on top of the handles, which kept them from bending. It was very hard work in the hot sun and instead of chanteying we pulled and rode down the brakes with cries of: "Heave and bust her! Heave and paul!" etc., until we could do nothing more. The bow was hove down about eighteen inches and the mate at last said: "Avast heaving! We'll let the tide do the rest."

There were only two feet of tidal rise in the bay, not much to count on, but it was on the flood and after waiting about an hour a squall from the west'ard came up and both anchors were tripped. Before we could clear them we drifted down towards the Dutch ship and to keep from fouling her we had to let go again much to the disgust of us all. We had a strenuous day of it and the mates finally decided to knock off work and try it again the next day.

There was no chanteying the next day as our work was mostly dipping one end of the cable around the other chain. The starboard anchor was finally cleared and catted and we held to the port through the night awaiting two new men to come off for the crew.

Sunday, March 25th, with a full crew and a light breeze from the west'ard, we were called to heave anchor again; and with good prospects of getting away we hove in the chain to *Blow ye Winds in the Morning.*

BLOW YE WINDS IN THE MORNING
CAPSTAN

Moderato
Solo

And now we are all load — ed and

I don't give a damn, With anch—or weighed and

haus—er made, we'll sail to Yan—kee land sing—ing,

Chorus

Blow ye winds in the morn—ing. Blow ye winds, hi-

o! We'll clear a—way the morn—ing dew,

Blow ye winds hi — o!

And now we are all loaded,
And I don't give a damn,
With anchor weighed and hawser made
We'll sail to Yankee land, singing,

Blow ye winds in the morning.
Blow ye winds, hi-o!

Blow Ye Winds in the Morning

We'll clear away the morning dew,
Blow ye winds, hi-o.

We are bound for New York City,
    In the good old ship *Akbar;*
The Old Man brought the consul out
    With a barrel of Stockholm tar, singing,

Oh, Java is the hottest place
    You ever saw for weather;
We dropped both anchors in the bay
    And hove them together, singing,

'Twas heave and pawl throughout the day,
    No headway did we gain.
The chains slipped down a tangled mess,
    We nearly went insane, singing,

Her bow hove down a foot or more
    Before the close of day,
The tide arose, the mud hooks broke,
    And so we sailed away, singing,

    S. B. Luce, in his *Naval Songs,* gives the same air but different words
in *The Merman.*

THE MERMAN

CAPSTAN

Tune: *Blow ye Winds in the Morning*

'Twas on Sunday morn and down
    Across the Southern Sea,
Our ship she laid at anchor
    And she waited for a breeze, singing,

Blow ye winds in the morning,
    Blow ye winds, hi-o
We'll clear away the morning dew,
    Blow ye winds, hi-o.

131

The captain was down below,
    And the men all laid about,
When under our bow we heard a splash,
    And then a regular shout, singing,

"Man overboard," the watchman cried
    And forward we all ran,
And hanging to the starboard chain
    Was an old bluff merman, singing,

His hair was blue, his eyes were green,
    His mouth was big as three,
His long green tail that he sat on,
    Went wigglin' in the sea, singing,

"Helloa!" cried our mate as bold as brass,
    "What cheer, messmate!" said he.
"Oh, I want to speak to your Old Man,
    I've a favor to ask, you see," singing,

"For I've been all night at a small sea fight
    At the bottom of the deep sea.
Oh, 'twould break your heart to hear them groan
    And the fun they've had with me," singing,

The Old Man then he came on deck,
    And looked on the waters blue,
"Come tell me my man, and as quick as you can,
    What favor can I do for you?" singing,

"Oh, you've dropped your anchor before my house
    And blocked up my only door,
And my wife can't get out, to roam about,
    Nor my chicks who number four," singing,

"The anchor shall be hove in at once,
    And your wife and your chicks set free;

But I never saw a scale, from a sprat to a whale,
    Till now, that could speak to me," singing,

"Your figurehead is like a sailor bold,
    And you speak like an Englishman,
But where did you get such a great big tail?
    Come, answer me that if you can," singing.

"A long time ago, from the ship *Hero*,
    I fell overboard in a gale,
And away down below, where the sea weeds grow,
    I met a lovely young girl—with a tail," singing,

"She saved my life and I made her my wife,
    And my legs changed instantly;
Now I am married, to a mermaid,
    At the bottom of the deep blue sea," singing,

Everybody being in good spirits, we proceeded to sing all the chanties and songs for a "Homeward Bounder" that could be remembered, among which was *Rolling Home*, started by Archie. This song is an English chantey, but being bound for New York, he changed the words in "Rolling Home to Fair England" to New York City, which Dick did not fancy, for he stamped his feet, shouting "Dear Old England!" while singing the chorus.

ROLLING HOME
CAPSTAN

Call all hands to man the cap-stan. See your

ca-bles are all clear; For to-night we weigh our an-chor, for A -

meri-ca's shore we'll steer. Heave a - way, now with a

will, boys, Ever-y hand you can clap on, As we walk a-round the

Chorus

cap-stan, you will hear that well known song. Roll - ing

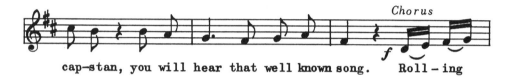

home, roll-ing home, Roll-ing home a-cross the sea; Roll-ing

home to New York Cit-y, roll-ing home, dear land, to thee.

Call all hands to the capstan,
  See your cables are all clear,
For tonight we weigh our anchor,
  For America's shore we'll steer.
Heave away, now, with a will, boys,
  Every hand you can clap on,
As we walk around the capstan,
  You will hear that well known song.

Rolling home, rolling home,
  Rolling home across the sea;
Rolling home to New York City,
  Rolling home, dear land, to thee.

Up aloft among the rigging,
    Blows the swift refreshing gale.
Heave away, now, with a will, boys,
    For the wind fills every sail.
Lay your topsails to the breeze, boys,
    Run your jibs high up the stay,
As we walk around the capstan,
    You will hear some sailor say,

To our fairest Java maidens,
    We will bid a fond adieu,
And we shall never forget you,
    For the days we spent with you.
Many thousand miles behind us,
    And we go ten thousand more,
Ere we reach our native country,
    Dear old New York, on America's shore.

Cheer up, Jack, bright smiles await you,
    Fond caresses from the fair;
Hearts and hands will ever meet you
    With kind welcomes everywhere.
And the girl we love so dearly,
    She, so loving, fond, and true,
Will clasp you to her bosom,
    And each tender word renew.

There are numerous versions both of words and music of this chantey. I give here the words by W. B. Whall.

ROLLING HOME II

Call all hands to man the capstan,
    See the cable runs down clear.
Heave away and with a will, boys,
    For old England we will steer.
And we'll sing in joyful chorus
    In the watches of the night,

And we'll sight the shores of England,
  When the gray dawn brings the light.

Rolling home, rolling home,
  Rolling home across the sea,
Rolling home to dear old England
  Rolling home, dear land, to thee.

Up aloft amid the rigging
  Blows the loud exulting gale.
Like a bird's wide outstretched pinions
  Spreads on high each swelling sail;
And the wild waves cleft behind us,
  Seem to murmur as they flow,
There are loving hearts that wait you
  In the land to which you go.

Many thousand miles behind us,
  Many thousand miles before,
Ancient ocean heaves to waft us
  To the well-remembered shore.
Cheer up, Jack, bright smiles await you
  From the fairest of the fair,
And her loving eyes will greet you
  With kind welcome everywhere.

Archie and Williams were soon with us and the clank of the windlass raised our spirits while we chantied another "Homeward Bounder."

OUTWARD BOUND
CAPSTAN

At Sou- ra - ba-ya town we'll bid a - dieu to

136

Outward Bound

love-ly Kate and pret-ty Sue; Our an-chor's weighed and our

Chorus

sail's un-furled, And we're bound to plough the water-y world, And

f say, "We're out-ward bound, Hur-rah! We're out-ward bound."

At Surabaya town we'll bid adieu
    To lovely Kate and pretty Sue;
Our anchor's weighed and our sails unfurled,
    And we're bound to plough the watery world.

And say, "We're outward bound,
Hurrah! We're outward bound."

The wind it blows from the no'no'theast,
    Ten knots our ship will make at least;
Our pirate guns and balls supply,
    And while we've powder we'll never say die.

And when we get to Malabar,
    Or some other port not quite so far,
Our captain will our wants supply,
    And while we've grub we'll never say die.

Then, at last our captain comes on board,
    Our sails are bent, we're manned and stored;
The jack is hoisted at the fore,
    Good-bye to the girls, we'll see them no more.

At last the man on the look out,
    Proclaims a sail with a joyful shout,

Handling the small (port) bower anchor on the bark *Alice*   (Mystic Seaport 1996. 113.1.22)

"Can you make her out?" "Yes, I think I can,
  She's a pilot standing out from land."

When we arrive in New York town,
  The pretty girls will flock around,
And these are the words you'll hear them say,
  "Oh, here comes Jack with his nine month's pay."

Then away to the sign of the Dog and Bell,
  'Tis there good cheer they always sell;
Mother Langly comes with her usual smile,
  Saying, "Go to it boys, it's worth your while!"

And when our money's all gone and spent,
  There's none to be borrowed and none to be lent,
Mother Langly comes with her usual frown,
  Saying, "Get up, Jack, let John sit down!"

Then poor old Jack must understand
  There's a ship in the dock that must be manned.
He goes on board as he's done before,
  And bids adieu to his native shore.

Then Tommy said, "Yous fellers have sung every thing from hell to breakfast. Before we get to New Yorek, why in the bloody hell don't yous give us 'Paddy woreks 'an the railway'." And so they did.

OH, POOR PADDY WORKS ON THE RAILWAY

CAPSTAN

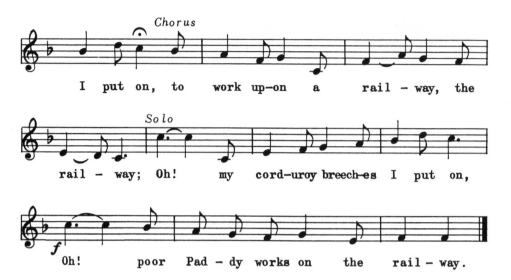

Chorus

I put on, to work up-on a rail - way, the

Solo

rail - way; Oh! my cord-uroy breech-es I put on,

Oh! poor Pad - dy works on the rail - way.

In eighteen hundred and forty-one,
  My corduroy breeches I put on.
Oh, my corduroy breeches I put on,
  To work upon a railway, the railway.

Oh! My corduroy breeches I put on,
Oh! Poor Paddy works on the railway.

In eighteen hundred and forty-two,
  I found I could no better do.
I found I could no better do,
  Than work upon a railway, the railway.

In eighteen hundred and forty-three,
  I thought I'd better cross the sea.
I thought I'd better cross the sea,
  To work upon a railway, the railway.

In eighteen hundred and forty-four,
  I landed on Columbia's shore.
I landed on Columbia's shore,
  To work upon a railway, the railway.

Oh, Poor Paddy Works on the Railway

In eighteen hundred and forty-five,
    I found myself more dead than alive,
I found myself more dead than alive,
    From working on a railway, the railway.

In eighteen hundred and forty-six,
    I found myself in a hell of a fix.
I found myself in a hell of a fix,
    From working on a railway, the railway.

In eighteen hundred and forty-seven,
    I wished myself from hell to heaven.
I wished myself from hell to heaven,
    From working on a railway, the railway.

In eighteen hundred and forty-eight,
    My boys, I'm sorry to relate,
My boys, I'm sorry to relate,
    That I worked on a railway, the railway.

In eighteen hundred and forty-nine,
    I then concluded to resign.
I then concluded to resign,
    From working on a railway, the railway.

In eighteen fifty I soon found,
    Myself shanghaied, for Frisco bound.
Myself shanghaied to Frisco bound,
    To work upon a railway, the railway.

The railway started me to roam,
    But the sea is hell and I can't get home,
But the sea is hell and I can't get home,
    To work upon a railway, the railway.

With the orders to set the main topsail, we began to chantey on all the sails, starting the main topsail with *So Handy, My Boys, So Handy*.

SO HANDY, MY BOYS, SO HANDY

HALLIARDS

Oh, shake her up from down below,
So handy, my boys, so handy.
Oh, shake her up and away we'll go.
So handy, my boys, so handy.

I'm Handy Jim from Bangor, Maine.
I courted a girl named Sarah Jane.

Sarah Jane was a kitchen maid,
And into her kitchen I often strayed.

But one fine night, through good luck or not,
The missus came home — in the copper I got.

I says to myself, "I'm a goner, God knows,
For the missus gave orders for washing the clothes."

The fire was kindled — the copper got hot,
And the missus she came for to stir up the pot.

142

So Handy, My Boys, So Handy

The missus she came for to stir up the pot,
When I jumped out, for 'twas then smoking hot.

The misses cried "Thief!" and for me she did run,
But I was away like the shot of a gun.

The missus came back — the devil's to pay,
For she gave the sack to Sarah next day.

Then Sarah she came to me quickly and cries,
"My character's lost! And my place likewise.

"Come, dry your eyes. Never mind," I said,
"Next Sunday morn we'll go and get wed."

Give one more pull before we belay,
The t'gan'sles are next and we'll chantey all day.

And up aloft this yard must go,
Stretch her leech and leave it so"[10]

Then with the main t'gan'sle, *I Love the Blue Mountains.*

I LOVE THE BLUE MOUNTAINS

HALLIARDS

Oh, I love the Blue Moun-tains; the Blue Moun-tains of Ten-nes-see, That's the place for you and me, I'm bound for Ten-nes-see.

Oh, I love the Blue Mountains,
The Blue Mountains of Tennessee.
That's the place for you and me,
I'm bound for Tennessee.

In eighteen hundred and sixty-three,
That's where my massa set me free.

My wife is there with her pickaninny,
And soon I'll have him upon my knee.

The ship sails free for you and me,
When I get there I'll quit the sea.

These words are of negro origin and different from those used by our crew.

ROLL THE COTTON DOWN
HALLIARDS

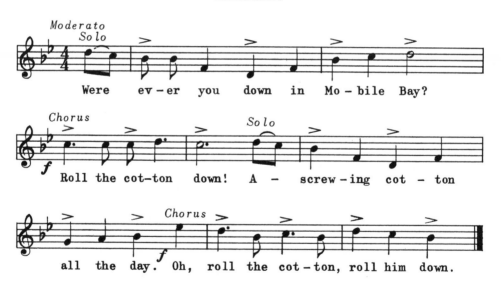

Were ever you down in Mobile Bay?
Roll the cotton down!
A-screwing cotton all the day,
Oh, roll the cotton, roll him down.

144

Five dollars a day is a white man's pay,
And the nigger works all night and day.

Away down south in Alabam',
Three square meals to the colored man.

We're loaded full in Mobile Bay,
At break of day we sail away.

We'll sail away across the sea,
But Mobile Bay is the place for me.

SONG OF THE FISHES[11]
HALLIARDS

I'll sing you a song of the fish in the sea, And trust that you'll join in the cho-rus with me. Then blow ye winds west - er - ly, west - er - ly blow - - We're bound to the south - 'ard, so stead - y we go.

I'll sing you a song of the fish in the sea,
And trust that you'll join in the chorus with me.

Then blow ye winds westerly, westerly blow,
We're bound to the south'ard, so steady we go.

The first was a flat fish, they call him a skate,
"If you are the cap'n, why then I'll be the mate."

And next comes the hake, who was black as a rook,
He said, "I'm no sailor, but I'll ship as the cook."

Then up comes a bluefish a-waggin' his tail,
He comes up on deck and yells, "All hands make sail!"

Then next come the eels, with their long nimble tails,
They jumped up aloft and loosed all the big sails.

And next comes the herrings, with their little tails,
They manned sheets and halliards and set all the sails.

Next comes the porpoise, with his short stubby snout,
He jumps on the poop and yells, "Ready about!"

And next comes the swordfish, the scourge of the sea.
The order he gives is, "Hellum's a-lee!"

And then comes the snapper as red as a beet,
And he shouts from the poop, "Oh, haul in the foresheet!"

And having accomplished these wonderful feats,
The black bass sings out next, to "raise tacks and sheets!"

Next comes the big whale and the largest of all,
And sings with a gruff voice, "Haul taut, mainsail haul!"

And then comes the mackerel, with his striped back,
He flopped about yelling, "Oh, board the main tack!"

And next comes the sprat, which is smallest of all,
He sings out, Haul well taut!' and "Let go and haul!"

And then comes the codfish, with his chuckle head,
Out on the main chains, for he's heaving the lead.

Next comes the flat flounder, quite fresh from the ground,
It's "Damn your eyes, chucklehead, mind where you sound!"

Along comes the dolphin a-flapping his tail,
He yelled to the boatswain to reef his foresail.

Along came the shark with his three rows of teeth,
He flops on the foreyard and takes a snug reef.

Then up jumps the fisherman, stalwart and grim,
He dipped in his big net and scooped them all in.

In light and baffling winds with intermittent squalls, we dropped our anchor twice during the afternoon to keep from grounding on the flats. The last squall drove us aground and we lowered all sails till the squall passed by. Then it was, "Man the windlass!" and Archie gave us an old chantey, *The Mermaid*.

THE MERMAID
CAPSTAN

One Fri – day morn when we set sail, and we

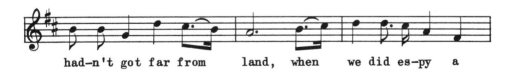

had–n't got far from land, when we did es–py a

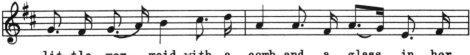

lit–tle mer – maid with a comb and a glass in her

One Friday morn when we set sail,
    And we hadn't got far from land,
When we did espy a little mermaid
    With a comb and a glass in her hand.
In her hand, with a comb and a glass in her hand.

Oh, the raging sea does roar, does roar,
    And the stormy winds how they blow.
While we poor sailors are laying up aloft,
    And the landlubbers lying down below.
Below, below, and the landlubbers lying down below.

148

Then up spoke the captain of our gallant ship
    And a jolly old captain was he.
"Oh, I have a wife in Salem town,
    But tonight a widow she will be."
Will be, will be, but tonight a widow she will be.

Then up spoke the mate of this gallant ship,
    And a bold young man was he.
"Oh, I've got a wife in New Bedford town,
    But a widow I fear she will be."
Will be, will be, but a widow I fear she will be.

Then up spoke the cook of our gallant ship,
    And a greasy old cook was he.
"I care more for my kettles and pans
    Than I do for the roaring sea."
The roaring sea, than I do for the roaring sea.

Then up spoke the cabin boy of our gallant ship,
    And a dirty little brat was he.
"Oh, I had a daddy up in Boston once,
    But he never cared a damn for me."
For me, for me, but he never cared a damn for me.

Then three times round went our gallant ship,
    And stuck up her nose, did she,
And the third time, settled as she turned around,
    And she sank to the bottom of the sea.
The sea, the sea, and she sank to the bottom of the sea.

There wasn't much of a hoist to the anchor and one song was enough. The topsails were hoisted with a song as usual and with the main t'gan'sle, Williams gave us an old timer, *A Hundred Years Ago*. Before the chantey ended the ship heeled over nicely and we shook the mud from our keel and were afloat again.

A HUNDRED YEARS AGO

HAND OVER HAND

A hun–dred years is a ve–ry long time.

Ho, yes, ho! A hun–dred years is a

ve–ry long time, A hun–dred years a – go.

A hundred years is a very long time.
Ho, yes, ho!
A hundred years is a very long time,
A hundred years ago.

A hundred years ago or more,
The world was square and such a bore.

Because they taught to every race,
Beyond the edge they'd fall in space.

A hundred years or more in jail,
Columbus said he'd surely sail.

A hundred years or more,
He sailed his ship to Columbia's shore.

A hundred years, it quickly flies,
Old England claimed she'd rule the seas.

A hundred years, in every clime,
The Stars and Stripes will float sublime.

150

In light, variable winds we only made about ten miles during the day and then anchored as the tide was on the ebb. Although we had a pilot aboard, the next day we grounded only ten miles from our former anchorage. With favorable cat's paws it was heave and chantey the greater part of the day. A fine breeze from the nor'ard springing up in the evening, being still aground, we hove up anchor and set all the sails, to no avail, for she was stuck hard and fast and wouldn't move. Finally we gave it up and furled the sails, letting go the anchor, waiting for the morning tide which floated us. There was no wind and we worked all day in a hot, boiling sun, kedging over the flats and singing all the songs at the capstan, I think, that were ever sung.

On March 29th the pilot left us at nine p.m. and we steered a course southeast by south in light winds and calms. The following morning we took in the longboat and the kedge anchor. Early on the morning of April 7th we passed through and were outside of Lombok Strait and got our anchors in and the chains stowed below. The good weather held until May 5th, when we were off the southern coast of Africa and sighted our first sail since leaving Java.

On May 13th, 1877, at noon, the Cape of Good Hope bore NNW, about forty-five miles away. We ran into a gale the next day and carried away the mizzen stay but no particular damage was done. After passing through the usual squalls we struck the southeast trades in lat. 20° S, long. 7° W. In light winds and very hot weather we sighted Wreck Hill, the westernmost part of Bermuda Island. The ship was now as clean as a yacht and we were all ready for Sandy Hook where we dropped anchor on the morning of July 19th, to await orders.

The next afternoon the tugboats *E. H. Coffin* and *A. F. Walcott* came down with the captain, with orders to proceed to Brooklyn. This put us in better spirits and we hove up our anchor for the last time to *Heave Away My Johnnies*.

> I heard our good chaplain palaver one day
> About souls, heaven, mercy, and such.
> And, my timbers! what lingo he'd coil and belay,
> Why, 'twas all one to me as High Dutch.

But he said how a sparrow can't flounder, d'ye see,
    Without orders that came down below,
And many a fine thing, that proved clearly to me
    That Providence takes us in tow.

For says he, "Do you mind, let storms e'er so oft
    Take the topsails of sailors aback,
There's a sweet little cherub that sits up aloft
    To keep watch o'er the life of poor Jack.

Bending a new fore upper topsail on the bark *Alice* (Mystic Seaport 1996.113.1.28)

Making music on the quarterdeck of the bark *Alice*
(Mystic Seaport 1996.113.1.61)

Chanties And Sea Songs

THERE ARE a great many chanties that I have never heard, and there are several books on chanties containing mere trash. One of the best publications is an English book by W. B. Whall, Master Mariner, entitled *Ships, Sea Songs and Shanties*, in which he gives a capstan chantey *Boston*, saying he had never met with it and its origin was unknown to him. It is evidently an American chantey, although it may have been composed by a Britisher, upon leaving Boston in the '60s. It is too good a chantey to die out and, although it will probably never be sung again by a ship's crew, I give it as rendered by Captain Whall. Holman Day mentions *Boston* in his *Blow the Main Down*.

BOSTON
CAPSTAN

From Bos-ton har-bor we set sail, when it was blow-ing a

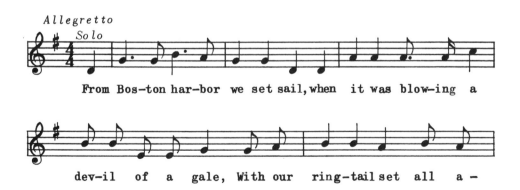

dev-il of a gale, With our ring-tail set all a —

baft the miz-zen peak, and our Yan-kee ship a-

Chorus

plow-ing up the deep, With a big Bow-wow!

Tow-row-row! Fal-de-ral de ri-do-day.

From Boston harbor we set sail,
    When it was blowing a devil of a gale,
With our rigging set all abaft the mizzen peak,
    And our Yankee ship a-ploughing up the deep,

With a big bow-wow! Tow-row row!
Fal-de-ral de ri-do-day.

Up comes the skipper from down below,
    And he looks aloft and he looks alow,
And he looks alow and he looks aloft,
    And it's "Coil up your ropes there, fore and aft."

Then down to his cabin he quickly crawls,
    And unto his steward he loudly bawls,
"Go fix me a glass that will make me cough,
    For it's better weather here than it is up aloft."

We poor sailors standing on the deck,
    With the blasted rain all a-pouring down our necks,
Not a drop of grog would he to us afford,
    But he damned our eyes at every other word.

Now the old beggar's dead and gone,
    Damn his eyes, he's left a son,

And if to us he doesn't prove frank,
  We'll very soon make him walk the plank.

And one thing which we have to prove,
  Is that he may have a watery grave.
So we'll heave him down into some dark hole,
  Where the sharks'll have his body and the devil'll have his soul.

In the *Boston* chantey I have taken the liberty to insert "Yankee Ship" where Captain Whall gives "Rule Britania."

Another chantey that I never heard was sung to me by Captain J. L. Botterill, an Englishman, who claimed it was sung as a walk away chantey on the four masted bark, *Samantha*. He could only remember the first verse. Through the courtesy of Mr. F. W. Siddall, editor of *Sea Breezes,* Liverpool, England, who asked for the song in the magazine, it appeared in the November 1935 issue as given by Capt. A. G. Cole of Languard, Isle of Wight.

The music, as sung by Capt. Botterill, is as follows:

THE BOS'UN'S STORY
WALK AWAY

"'Tis a hun-dred years," said the bo'-sun bold, "since I was a boy at sea. 'Tis a hun-dred years, so I've been told, and that's the truth," said he. "And that's the truth," said

he. "We sailed a-way from Mil-ford Bay, the North Pole for to

see; And we found it too with-out much a - do,

And that's the truth," said he. "And that's the truth," said he.

"'Tis a hundred years," said the bo'sun bold,
   "Since I was a boy at sea.
'Tis a hundred years, so I've been told,
   And that's the truth," said he.
   And that's the truth, said he.
"We sail away from Milford Bay,
   The North Pole for to see;
And we found it too without much ado,
   And that's the truth," said he.
   And that's the truth said he.

"We sailed and sailed, and one fair noon
   A great whale we espied.
So we took a rope and a long harpoon,
   And stuck him in the starboard side.
Then away and away went the great big whale,
   And away and away went we.
Made fast to his tail to the north we did sail,
   And that's the truth," said he.

"When we came to the great North Star,
   An iceberg we did see.
Said the captain, 'Now we have come thus far,
   I am not going back,' said he.

So we tickled the tail of the great big whale
  With a tenpenny nail, did we.
And we sailed right through that iceberg blue,
  And that's the truth," said he.

"And then the North Pole we did see,
  And we anchored the whale astarn,
But he gave us a whack that sent us back,
  Or I mightn't have been spinning this yarn.
So messmates all," said the bo'sun bold,
  "If the North Pole you would see,
You've got to sail at the tail of a whale,
  And that's the truth," said he.

NANCY LEE
CAPSTAN

Stephan Adams

there she stands and waves her hand up-on the quay, And

ev-'ry day when I'm a-way, she'll watch for me, And

Chorus

whis-per low, when tem-pests blow, for Jack at sea. Yeo

ho! Lads ho! Yeo ho! The

sail-or's wife the sail-or's star shall be. Yeo

ho! We go a-cross the sea. The

sail-or's wife the sail-or's star shall be, The

sail-or's wife, his star shall be.

Nancy Lee

Of all the wives as e'er you know,
    Yeo ho! Lads ho! Yeo ho! Yeo ho!
There's none like Nancy Lee, I know,
    Yeo ho! Lads ho! Yeo ho! Yeo ho!
See there she stands and waves her hand upon the quay,
    And every day when I'm away she'll watch for me,
And whisper low, when tempests blow, for Jack at sea.
    Yeo ho! Lads ho! Yeo ho!

The sailor's wife the sailor's star shall be.
    Yeo ho! We go across the sea.
The sailor's wife the sailor's star shall be,
    The sailor's wife, his star shall be.

The harbor's past, the breezes blow,
    'Tis long ere we come back, I know.
But true and bright from morn till night my home will be,
    And all so neat and snug and sweet, for Jack at sea,
And Nancy's face to bless the place, and welcome me.

The bo'sun pipes the watch below,
    Then here's a health afore we go,
A long, long life to my sweet wife, and mates at sea,
    And keep our bones from Davy Jones, where-e'er we be!
And may you meet a mate as sweet as Nancy Lee.

HIGH BARBAREE

CAPSTAN

There were two loft-y ships from Old Eng-land came.

came. Blow high! Blow low! And so sail-ed

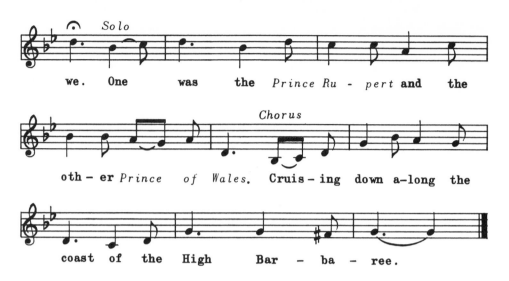

we. One was the Prince Ru - pert and the

oth - er Prince of Wales. Cruis - ing down a-long the

coast of the High Bar - ba - ree.

There were two lofty ships from Old England came.
  Blow high! Blow low! And so sailed we.
One was the *Prince Rupert* and the other *Prince of Wales*,
  Cruising down along the coast of the High Barbaree.

"Aloft! Aloft!" our jolly bo'sun cries,
"Look ahead, look astern, look a-weather and a-lee."

There's none upon the stern, there's none upon the lee,
But there's a lofty ship to windward, she is sailing fast and free.

"Oh, hail her! Oh, hail her!" our gallant captain cried,
"Are you man-of-war or a privateer," said he.

"Oh, I am no man-of-war, no privateer," said she,
"But I am a salt-sea pirate, a-looking for my fee!"

"If you are a jolly pirate, I'd have you come this way,
Bring out your quarter-guns, boys, we'll show these pirates play."

'Twas broadside to broadside, a long time they lay,
Until the *Prince Rupert* shot the pirate's mast away.

"Oh, quarter! Oh, quarter!" these pirates did cry,
But the quarters that we gave them — we sank them in the sea.

I have never heard this song sung as a chantey, but other writers say it was so sung. In the seventh verse, S. B. Luce gaves the name "Prince Rupert," W. B. Whall uses "Prince Luther," Joanna C. Colcord, "Prince of Wales." She states that the original of *High Barbaree* can be found in *The Sea's Anthology* by Patterson, under the title, *The Sayler's Onely Delight*."

ALONG THE LOWLANDS
CAPSTAN

Allegretto
Solo

We're sail-ing in a coast-er a - long the low-land shore, but

soon we'll join a Yank-ee ship to sail the o-cean o'er. For

schoon-ers and the brigs, all the shoals and reefs they fear, but

Chorus

big ships keep a-way from land, in safe-ty as they steer. Now we

sail a-long the low - lands, low-lands, low - lands. But we

soon shall leave the shelt - ered shore, And a -

way from all the low - lands, low - lands,

low - lands, We will sail the deep blue o - cean o'er.

We're sailing in a coaster along the lowland shore,
    But soon we'll join a Yankee ship to sail the ocean o'er.
For schooners and the brigs, all the shoals and reefs they fear,
    But the big ships keep away from land, in safety as they steer.

Now we sail along the lowlands, lowlands, lowlands.
    But we soon shall leave the sheltered shore,
And away from all the lowlands, lowlands, lowlands,
    We will sail the deep blue ocean o'er.

And now we've left the lowlands and we are bound to sea,
    The wind may blow a living gale — it matters not to me.
Our anchor's in, and cable stowed in locker down below,
    We're sailing far away from shoals along the lowlands low.

Luce's *Naval Songs* gives different words under *Sailing by the Lowlands.*

BARNACLE BILL THE SAILOR
PUMPS

Moderato
Solo

"Who's that knock - ing at the door?" asked the

Barnacle Bill the Sailor

fair young maid-en. "It's on-ly me from o-ver the

sea." Said Barn-a - cle Bill the sail-or.

"Who's that knocking at the door?"
  Asked the fair young maiden.
"It's only me from over the sea,"
  Said Barnacle Bill the sailor.

"What do you want, I'd like to know?"
  Asked the fair young maiden.
"I'll break down the door. Don't wait any more!"
  Said Barnacle Bill the sailor.

"I'll come down and let you in,"
  Said the fair young maiden.
"Make up your bed new, and make it for two!"
  Said Barnacle Bill the sailor.

"What if they should call the cops?"
  Asked the fair young maiden.
"Oh bugger the cops, the sons of Wops,"
  Said Barnacle Bill the sailor.

"What if we should have a child?"
  Asked the fair young maiden.
"I'd make it a wreck, for I'd wring its neck!"
  Said Barnacle Bill the sailor.

"When will I see you again?"
  Asked the fair young maiden.

"Oh, never no more, for I sail the seas o'er,"
Said Barnacle Bill the sailor.

This pumping chantey is similar to *Abel Brown, the Sailor,* in its words, and follows along the same channel, too coarse for print as sung in days gone by.

Miss Colcord, in her *Roll and Go,* says: "There was always a set of verses embodying the original idea, which was perfectly fit to print, with perhaps one exception, the notorious *Abel Brown,* of which there is no version in any of the published collections I have examined."

I doubt very much if *this* song was ever in print, but it was a popular pumping chantey in early days and is typical of the drunken sailor ashore going out to "paint the town red."

THE PRIEST AND THE NUNS
PUMPS

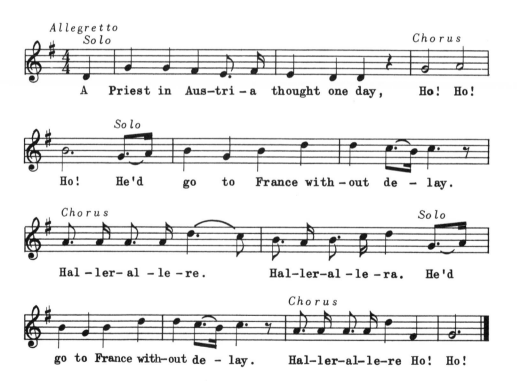

The Priest and the Nuns

A priest in Austria thought one day,
  Ho! Ho! Ho!
He'd go to France without delay.
  Hal-ler-al-le-re. Hal-ler-al-le-ra.
He'd go to France without delay.
  Hal-ler-al-le-re Ho! Ho!

So when the father came to France,
'Twas seven sick nuns he found by chance.

He saw these nuns in a convent yard,
All lying down on benches hard.

He gave these nuns his calling card,
And asked, "May I come in the yard?"

To one he asked what he could do,
"I'm priest as well as doctor too."

A sick nun then in quick reply
Said, "Treat me, Father, ere I die."

With cane in hand (a walking stick)
He touched the nun so very sick.

The others quickly ran to see,
And asked the priest, "What could it be?"

"A medicine stick in my hand I hold
To cure all sick nuns in my fold."

Another nun that laid close by
Cried, "Father, none so sick as I."

He treated all the nuns alike
And said he'd call another night.

Their money gone, they looked in vain
For the priest that carried a walking cane.

167

DO ME AMA

PUMPS

As Jack was walk-ing through the square, He

met a la-dy and a squire. Now,

Jack he heard the squire say, "To-night with you I mean to stay."

Do me a-ma din-ghy a-ma, do me a-ma day.

As Jack was walking through the square,
 He met a lady and a squire.
Now Jack, he heard the squire say,
 "Tonight with you I mean to stay."
Do me ama dinghy ama,
 Do me ama day.

"I will tie a string to my little finger,
 And the other end hang out the window.
Then you must come and pull the string;
 I'll come down and let you in."

"Damn my eyes," says Jack, "if I do not venture
 For to pull the string hanging out of the window."
So Jack he went and pulled the string;
 She came down and let him in.

168

"Oh, what is that which smells so tarry?
    I've nothing in the house that's tarry."
"It's a tarry sailor down below.
    Kick him out — in the snow."

"Oh, what d'you want, you tarry sailor?
    You've come to rob me of my treasure!"
"Oh no," says Jack, "I pulled the string;
    You came down and let me in."

This song of Whall's is a good companion to *Barnacle Bill the Sailor*.

ADIEU TO MAIMUNA

CAPSTAN

The boat-men shout, 'tis time to part, No long-er can we

stay.   'Twas then Ma-i-mu-na taught my heart how

much a glance can say.   'Twas then Ma-i-mu-na

taught my heart how much a glance can say.

The boatmen shout, 'tis time to part,
    No longer can we stay.
'Twas then Maimuna taught my heart

169

How much a glance can say.
'Twas then Maimuna taught my heart
How much a glance can say.

With trembling steps to me she came.
Farewell, she would have cried.
But ere her lips the words could frame,
In half-framed sounds it died.
But ere her lips the words could frame,
In half-framed sounds it died.

Through tear-dimn'd eyes beamed looks of love,
Her arms around me flung,
As clings the breeze on sighing grieve,
Upon my breast she clung.
As clings the breeze on sighing grieve,
Upon my breast she clung.

My willing arms embraced the maid,
My heart with rapture beat.
While she but wept the more and said,
"Would we had never met."
While she but wept the more and said,
"Would we had never met."

This was sung as a chantey in American ships in the early fifties.

No book of chanties can be complete without *Let go the Reefy Tackle*. While strictly speaking this song is not a chantey, all old-time sailors will at once recognize the yarn of the stuttering Swede who had straddled the yardarm and was caught by the reef tackle. In pain he sang out to the mate on deck, but as he stuttered, words failed him. Whereupon the mate impatiently answered back, "If you can't tell what you want, sing it!" and this was his song—

LET GO THE REEFY TACKLE

Let go the reef-y tack-le! Reef tack - le, reef

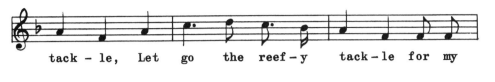

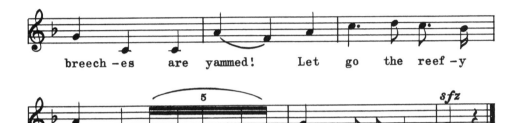

Let go the reefy tackle, reef tackle, reef tackle,
Let go the reefy tackle, for my breeches are *yammed!*
My breeches are yammed! My breeches are yammed!
Let go the reefy tackle,
For my breeches are yammed in the sheet block!

I heard a little song when Japanese sailors were taking supplies aboard the *Yokohama Maru* at Seattle. There were fifty or more sacks of spuds to be taken on. Two sailors picked up a sack (one at each end) and with a song, raised and swung it upon the shoulder of a third. On the last word of the song, *sa*, it was on his shoulder and he was off at a trot across the gang plank.

JAPANESE SHORT DRAG

Yoya sano *sa!*

171

THE PIRATE OF THE ISLE

Sung by Wm. R. B. Dawson, an old-time chanteyman.

Oh, I com-mand a stur-dy band of pi-rates bold and free. No laws I own, my ship's my throne, my king-dom is the sea. My flag is red at my mast-head, at all my foes I smile. I no quar-ter show where e'er I go, but soon the prize we'll take in tow, For my men are tried, my bark's my pride, my men are tried, my bark's my pride, I am the pi-rate of the isles, I'm the

The Pirate of the Isle

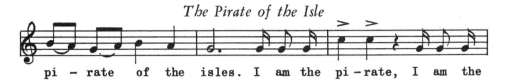

pi — rate of the isles. I am the pi — rate, I am the

pi — rate, I am the pi — rate of the isles.

Oh, I command a sturdy band
    Of pirates bold and free.
No laws I own, my ship's my throne,
    My kingdom is the sea.
My flag is red at my masthead,
    At all my foes I smile.
I no quarter show where e'er I go,
    But soon the prize we'll take in tow.

For my men are tried, my bark's my pride,
    My men are tried, my bark's my pride,
I'm the pirate of the isles,
    I'm the pirate of the isles.
I am the pirate, I am the pirate,
    I am the pirate of the isles.

I love to sail in a pleasant gale
    Across a deep and boundless sea.
With a prize in view (We'll take her too)
    And haul her under our lee.
Then give three cheers and homeward steer,
    Let fortune on us smile.
For none dare cross the famed Le Ross.
    (But soon his sail they stopped, of course.)

Proud Gallia's sons and Spanish dons
    With ardent yellow burned.
They crossed the sea to capture me,
    But they never back returned.
Old England too, doth me pursue,
    At all her threats I gain.

Eight ships obtained, their men I've slain,
I've burnt and sunk them on the main.

But now in sight a ship of might
A British seventy-four;
She hails Le Ross and stops his course,
And broadside on him pours.
The pirate soon returns the boon,
And proudly does he smile,
But a fatal ball soon causes his fall,
And now his men for quarter call.

Final chorus:
In the briny deep he's laid to sleep.
In the briny deep he's laid to sleep.
He was the pirate of the Isles,
He was the pirate of the Isles.
He was the pirate, he was the pirate,
He was the pirate of the Isles.

MARRIED TO A MERMAID
Capstan

English

There was a gay young farm—er, Who lived on Salis—bury plain. He loved a rich knight's daugh—ter dear and she loved him a—gain. But the knight he was dis—

Married to a Mermaid

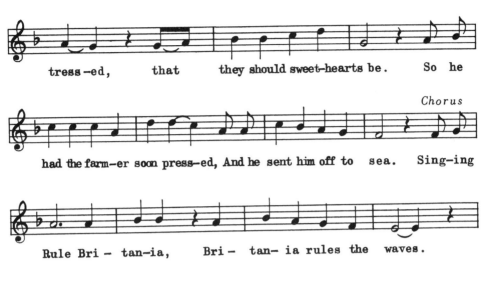

tress—ed, that they should sweet-hearts be. So he

Chorus

had the farm-er soon press-ed, And he sent him off to sea. Sing-ing

Rule Bri - tan-ia, Bri - tan- ia rules the waves.

Bri-tons nev-er nev- er nev - er will be slaves.

There was a gay young farmer,
  Who lived on Salisbury plain.
He loved a rich knight's daughter dear,
  And she loved him again.
But the knight he was distressed
  That they should sweethearts be,
So he had the farmer pressed
  And he sent him off to sea.
Singing rule, Britania, Britania rules the waves;
Britons never never never will be slaves.

Oh, 'twas on the deep Atlantic,
  Midst equinoctial gales,
This young farmer fell overboard,
  Among the sharks and whales.
He disappeared so quickly,
  So headlong down went he,

175

That he went out of sight like a streak of light
    To the bottom of the deep blue sea.

We lowered a boat to find him,
    No thought to find his corpse.
When up to the top he came with a bang
    And sang in a voice so hoarse:
"My comrades and my messmates,
    Oh, do not weep for me,
For I am married to a mermaid
    At the bottom of the deep blue sea."

He told us when he first went down
    The fish all came round he,
And they seemed to think as he did wink
    That he was rather free.
But down he went tho' he didn't know how,
    Saying, "It's all up with me."
When he came to a lovely mermaid
    At the bottom of the deep blue sea.

She raised herself on her beautiful tail
    And gave him her wet white hand,
Saying, "Long have I waited for you, my dear,
    You are welcome safe to land.
Go back to your messmates for the last time
    And tell them all for me,
That you are married to a mermaid
    At the bottom of the deep blue sea."

The wind was fair, the sails were set,
    And the ship was running free,
When we went up to our captain bold,
    And this we told to he.
Then the captain came to the old ship's side,
    And loudly bellowed he,
"Be as happy as you can with your wife, my man,
    At the bottom of the deep blue sea."

THE YANKEE MAN-OF-WAR

'Tis of a state-ly South-ern-er that flew the stripes and stars, And the whis-tling winds from the west-nor' west blew through her pitch-pine spars. With her star-board tacks a-board, my boys, she hung up-on the gale. On an au-tomn night we raised the light of the Old Head of Kin-sale.

'Tis of a stately southerner
    That flew the stripes and stars,
And the whistling winds from the west nor'west
    Blew through the pitchpine spars.
With her starboard tacks aboard, my boys,
    She hung upon the gale.
On an autumn night we raised the light
    Of the Old Head of Kinsale.

It was a clear and cloudless night
    And the wind blew steady and strong,
As gaily over the bounding deep
    Our good ship bowled along.
With the foaming seas beneath her bows
    The fiery waves she spread,
And bending low her bosom of snow
    She buried her lee cathead.

There was no talk of shortening sail
    From him who walked the poop,
And under the press of her ponderous jib,
    The boom bent like a hoop.
Her groaning chest tree told the strain
    That held her stout main tack,
But he only laughed as he glanced abaft
    At her bright and foaming track.

The mid tide meets the channel waves
    That flow from shore to shore,
And the mist hung heavy upon the land
    From Featherstone to Dunmore;
And the sterling light on Tuskar Rock
    Where the old bell tolls each hour,
And the beacon light that shone so bright
    Was quenched on Waterford Tower.

The nightly robes our good ship wore
    Were her whole topsails three;
Her spanker and her standing jib,
    The courses being free.
"Now lay aloft! my heroes bold,
    Not a moment must be passed,"
And royals and topgallant sails
    Were quickly on each mast.

What looms upon our starboard bow?
    What hangs upon the breeze?

'Tis time our good ship hauled her wind
    Abreast the Old Saltee's;
For by her ponderous press of sail
    And by her consorts four,
We saw our morning visitor
    Was a British man-of-war.

Up spake our noble captain then,
    As a shot ahead of us passed;
"Haul snug your flowing courses!
    Lay your topsail to the mast!"
Those Englishmen gave three loud hurrahs
    From the deck of their covered ark,
And we answered back by a solid broadside
    From the decks of our patriot ark.

Now, though we'd rather fight than run,
    We dared not risk defeat
Before the guns of that three-decked ark
    That led the British fleet.
She came rolling down on our weather beam
    With the white foam at her bow,
Out booms on board the Southerner
    Spare not the canvas now.

"Out booms! Out booms!" our skipper cried,
    "Out booms and give her sheet!"
And the swiftest keel that ever was launched
    Shot ahead of the British fleet.
And amidst a thundering shower of shot
    With stun'sails hoisting away,
Down the North Channel Paul Jones did steer
    Just at the break of day.

During the first war with England the achievements of other naval captains were eclipsed by those of John Paul Jones, a Scotch sailor who had settled in Virginia in 1773, and who, at the outbreak of the war, offered his services to Congress.

In 1778 he was sent with the 18 gun ship *Ranger* to prowl about the British coast. He entered the Irish Channel, seized the *Lord Chatham*, set fire to the shipping at Whitehaven, and captured the 20 gun sloop *Drake* after a fierce fight. In cruising about the British coasts so much damage was inflicted on shipping that Paul Jones became a sort of bogey to all England.

The *Yankee Man-of-War* is considered one of the very best of American sea songs. The author's name is unknown but it is believed that he was one of the crew of the *Ranger* which escaped from a British squadron in the Irish Channel in 1778.

It is one of the gems of the forecastle and has the full scent of the brine and the gale. There are several sets of words to the song.

Wm. R. B. Dawson, an old-time chanteyman and rigger, gave me a version as follows:

THE YANKEE MAN-OF-WAR II

"What's that! What's that on the starboard bow?"
From our masthead descried;
"It is an English man-of-war."
Our gallant captain cried.
"Bear down! Bear down on his port bow
And we'll give to him a broadside,
And we'll let him know that Paul Jones
Still rules king of the Irish tide.

'Twas eleven o'clock in the forenoon
We ranged up alongside,
Locked yardarm and yardarm,
Our foes we then descried.
"Come on! Come on you cowardly curs!"
Was heard above the din.
"If you have brass for outward show,
We've got good steel within."

For five long hours the battle raged,
'Twas furious and fast.

Paul Jones he led us in the van,
    We conquered them at last.
'Twas four o'clock in the afternoon
    The English flag rolled down;
"Well done, my boys!" Paul Jones he cried,
    " 'Tis a battle of renown."

THE SHIP LORD WOLSELEY

Tune: *Yankee Man-of-War*   Wm. R. B. Dawson

'Twas of a stately Irish ship
    That sailed the western seas,
Her name it was the *Lord Wolseley*,
    We sailed from Belfast quays.
Her captain's name was James Dunn,
    A man of courage bold,
With a crew of brave seamen as ever
    Sailed for honor and gold.

On the eighteenth day of January
    Our good ship left the land
We steered her down the North Channel
    For Philadelphia bound.
The wind was in our favor
    And we set all sail with glee;
Our hearts being light, our spirits bright,
    No thought of fail had we.

Now the watch is picked and the watch is set,
    Our spirits to revive.
Each cracked a joke or told a tale
    Of sweethearts or of wives.
While some told pleasant stories
    Of friends they'd ne'er see more,
With a heaven's blest, each dear kind friend
    Along the shamrock's shore.

181

On the evening of the nineteenth
 The wind blew fresh and strong;
"All hands save ship!" our captain cried,
 The word was passed along,
"Clew up and lower topgallant sails!
 Your upper topsails too!
Haul up your crossjack and courses!
 Haul down your jibs, boys, do!"

Our mate, a gallant and noble man,
 He led us in the van,
With his second and third officers,
 Both able to a man.
Our bo'sun and fourth officer,
 With their brave crew to back,
We snugged her down that fearful night;
 It was both drear and black.

The wind it blew out furiously,
 It being a tremendous gale;
To see our good ship laboring
 Caused stoutest hearts to quail.
To save her from a lee shore
 We toiled with willing hands;
"Well done, my boys!" our captain cried.
 "She bears up off the land."

Now for a harbor or safe roadstead,
 'Cross channel our good ship sped,
On the morning of the twentieth
 We raised Old Barra Head.
And then, into Loch Eynort,
 All on that rock-bound shore;
We thought we'd safely anchor,
 For our men were sick and sore.

But quickly from our anchorage
 We had then to retreat,

The Ship Lord Wolseley

And next to Loch Boisdale,
    Fresh dangers there to meet.
And thence to Stornoway we steered,
    Where success our efforts crowned;
Next day to sea we sailed away,
    Our good ship safe and sound.

Here's health to our commander
    And his officers so brave,
Along with our ship's company
    They thrice our ship did save.
And now we're sailing the ocean wide,
    Philadelphia bound once more,
Where Irish sons are welcome
    On that green and fertile shore.

In Philadelphia now at rest,
    Where we can go ashore;
After a long and stormy voyage
    Our troubles all are o'er.
When we return again, my boys,
    They'll greet us with a smile
With a hundred thousand welcomes,
    Back to Old Erin's Isle.

Dawson was bo'sun on the *Lord Wolseley* on this voyage where he composed the above. She was a four-masted ship of 3,000 tons, built by Harland and Wolff at Belfast in 1883 for the Lord Line of that city, and registered 2,518 tons. In 1903, as the German four-masted bark *Columbia* she was dismasted off Cape Flattery, salvaged, and towed into Victoria, British Columbia, where she again assumed her original name of *Lord Wolseley* and the British registry. Later she was bought by American interests and rigged as a six-masted barkentine. The mizzen mast of the *Wolseley* became the foremast of the *Everett G. Griggs*, the new name of the *Wolseley*. With a diminished spread of canvas, her crew was reduced from 55 to 17 hands, all told. She was capable of carrying two and a half million feet of lumber.

In 1910 the old vessel again changed hands when she was bought by Captain E. R. Sterling of Seattle, Washington, and given the name *E. R. Sterling.*

On April 16, 1927, the *Sterling* left Adelaide, Australia, with a cargo of grain for Falmouth, England. With adverse winds, she reached lat. 16° N, long. 30° 20' W, where on October 6th, in a violent gale, she was again dismasted and hobbled into St. Thomas, Virgin Islands, West Indies, on the 15th, just six months after leaving Adelaide. It was found impossible to re-rig the vessel there, so the owner decided that she should be towed to destination, a distance of 3,500 miles. The powerful tug *Indus* from Rotterdam began the tow from St. Thomas on December 15th, 1927, and finally reached her destination. Her bones are probably at rest in Falmouth.

Dawson said of the *Wolseley* on her maiden voyage, "The running rigging was of hemp. No sooner were we outside when it turned extremely cold with a rising gale. With orders to shorten sail, the hemp rigging was frozen stiff and refused to run through the blocks. It was impossible to get the sails off of her. So she was 'put before it' up the channel. She was the first ship I was ever in that ran away with me."

THE CONSTITUTION AND THE GUERRIERE

It oft-times has been told, that the Brit-ish sea-men

bold Could flog the tars of France so neat and han-dy,

oh! But they nev-er found their match, 'til the Yan-kees did them

catch, Oh, the Yan—kee boys for fight—ing are the dan—dy, oh!

It ofttimes has been told,
  That the British seamen bold
Could flog the tars of France so neat and handy, oh!
But they never found their match,
  'Til the Yankees did them catch,
Oh, the Yankee boys for fighting are the dandy, oh!

The *Guerriere* a frigate bold,
  On the foaming ocean rolled,
Commanded by proud Dacres the grandee, oh!
With as choice a British crew
  As a rammer ever drew,
Could flog the Frenchmen two to one so handy, oh!

When this frigate hove in view
  Said proud Dacres to his crew,
"Come, clear the ship for action and be handy, oh!
To the weather gauge, boys, get her,"
  And to make his men fight better,
Gave them to drink gunpowder mixed with brandy, oh!

Then Dacres loudly cries,
  "Make this Yankee ship your prize.
You can in thirty minutes neat and handy, oh!
Twenty-five's enough I'm sure,
  And if you'll do it in a score,
I'll treat you to a double share of brandy, oh!"

The British shot flew hot,
  Which the Yankees answered not,
'Til they got within the distance they called handy, oh!
"Now," says Hull to his crew,

"Boys, let's see what you can do,
If we take this boasting Briton we're the dandy, oh!"

The first broadside we poured
    Carried her mainmast by the board,
Which made the lofty frigate look abandoned, oh!
Then Dacres shook his head,
    And to his officers he said,
"Lord — I didn't think those Yankees were so handy, oh!"

Our second told so well
    That their fore and mizzen fell
Which doused the royal ensign all so handy, oh!
"By George," says he, "we're done!"
    And he fired a lee gun,
While the Yankee struck up Yankee Doodle Dandy, oh!

Then Dacres came on board
    To deliver up his sword,
Tho' loath was he to part with it, it was so handy, oh!
"Oh, keep your sword," says Hull,
    "For it only makes you dull,
Cheer up and let us have a little brandy, oh!"

Come fill your glasses full,
    And we'll drink to Captain Hull,
And so merrily we'll push about the brandy, oh!
John Bull may boast his fill,
    Let the world say what it will,
But the Yankee boys for fighting are the dandy, oh!

The music as we sang it when I was a boy, is about the same as that given by S. B. Luce, in his *Naval Songs*. He says, "This famous fight occurred August 19, 1812, off the New England coast. In twenty-five minutes the *Guerriere*, commanded by James R. Dacres, was totally dismasted and her hull so riddled that she was not thought worth towing into port, and was blown up. The *Constitution* was commanded by Captain Isaac Hull. Loss on *Constitution*, seven killed and wounded.

The fine seamanship, and the fighting capacity on the part of Hull was the theme of the best and most spirited song of the war. One which still keeps its place in the forecastle, and, it may be hoped, will keep it so long as Uncle Sam has a warship afloat.

The Englishmen celebrated their one signal victory of the war — the capture of the *Chesapeake* by the *Shannon* off Boston Light a year later — by a parody of this song, of a decidedly inferior quality.

SHANNON AND CHESAPEAKE

From W. B. Whall's *Ships, Sea-songs and Shanteys.*

Now the Ches-a-peake so bold, sailed from Bos-ton, we've been

told, for to take the Brit-ish frig-ate neat and han-dy,

Oh! The peo-ple in the port all came out to see the

sport, and the bands were play-ing Yan-kee Doo-dle Dan-dy, oh!

Now the *Chesapeake* so bold,
　　Sailed from Boston, we've been told,
For to take the British frigate neat and handy, oh!
The people in the port
　　All came out to see the sport,
And the bands were playing Yankee Doodle Dandy, oh!

The British frigate's name,
    Which for the purpose came
To cool the Yankee courage neat and handy, oh!
Was the *Shannon* — Captain Broke,
    All her men were hearts of oak
And at fighting were allowed to be dandy, oh!

'Twas before the fight begun
    That the Yankees with much fun,
Said, "We'll tow her into Boston neat and handy, oh!
And I'll 'kalkilate' we'll dine
    With our lasses drinking wine,
And we'll dance the jig of Yankee Doodle Dandy, oh!"

But the fight had scarce begun
    Ere they flinched from their guns,
Which at first they started working neat and handy, oh!
Then brave Broke he waved his sword,
    Crying, "Now, my lads, aboard,
And we'll stop their playing Yankee Doodle Dandy, oh!"

They no sooner heard the word
    Than they quickly jumped aboard,
And hauled down the Yankee colours neat and handy, oh!
Notwithstanding all their brag,
    Now the glorious flag
At the Yankee mizzen peak was quite the dandy, oh!

Here's a health, brave Broke, to you,
    To your officers and crew,
Who aboard the *Shannon* frigate fought so handy, oh!
And may it always prove
    That in fighting and in love,
The British tar for ever is the dandy, oh!

YANKEE TARS

From S. B. Luce's *Naval Songs*

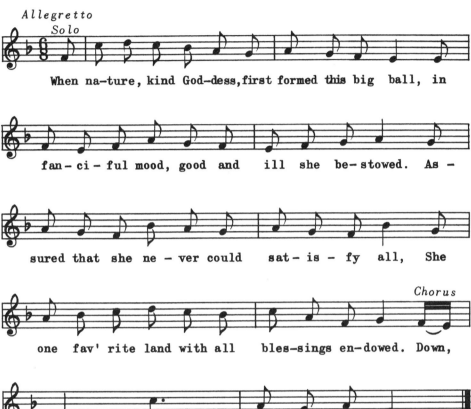

Allegretto

Solo

When na-ture, kind God-dess, first formed this big ball, in

fan-ci-ful mood, good and ill she be-stowed. As-

sured that she ne-ver could sat-is-fy all, She

Chorus

one fav' rite land with all bles-sings en-dowed. Down,

down, down, down, der-ry down.

When nature, kind goddess, first formed this big ball,
  In fanciful mood, good and ill she bestowed.
Assured that she never could satisfy all,
  She one fav'rite land with all blessings endowed.
Down, down, down, down, derry down.

She, its Columbia, that swore before Jove,
  That the rest of the world for this country should toil;
Through Asia and Africa and Europe her love
  Sought for us precious gifts from each clime and each soil.

189

Our country she made the asylum of love—
    The refuge of Liberty, Science and Arts,
Then as surely for truth and humanity's cause,
    She planted our bosoms with true Yankee hearts.

She then with these words made the welkin to ring,
    "You have now every blessing that I can bestow,
'Tis yours to preserve, and a Navy's the thing
    That your rights shall protect from each insolent foe."

She said — and 'twas done; then the Barbary shore
    Saw such daring as rival'd antiquity's name;
But the war for the rights of our tars gives once more
    To our tars a fair field to outdo ancient fame.

See the cruisers of Britain with threatening air
    Sweep the seas and defy us with thundering noise;
The *Guerriere* her name on her mainsail so fair,
    Cries, "Death or submission to all Yankee tars."

But Brave Captain Hull and his bold Yankee tars,
    Proved her masts were all heartless and heartless her men;
And the *Guerriere* soon bade a farewell to all wars,
    Justice triumphed! and justice shall triumph again!

The hero of Tripoli next met the foe,
    And 'tis still the same story told over again;
Of fighting, they scarcely could make out a show,
    When their masts were all gone, killed or wounded their men.

'Tis thus Yankee tars shall their country protect,
    And their rights on the seas on a sure basis place;
The vauntings and threat'nings of Britain be checked,
    And a Navy and commerce our country shall grace.

NANTUCKET P'INT

An old-timer that used to be sung
by the coast fishermen.

New York *Sun*

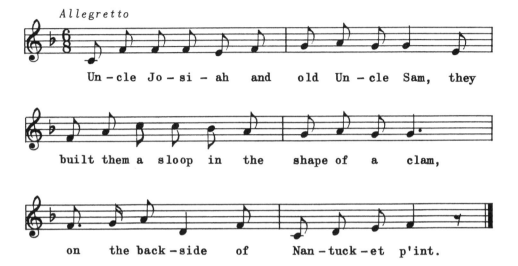

Uncle Josiah and old Uncle Sam,
They built them a sloop in the shape of a clam,
On the backside of Nantucket p'int.

They soon had her calked up both tight and staunch,
And when it was done she was ready to launch.

Then Uncle Josiah says he, "Sam, come,
You go up to the town for a runlet of rum."

Now at launching time there always is fun,
So down to the beach all the women do run.

There was Aunt Kesiah and Sally Pease
And Tabitha Bunker and Abigail Keyes.

And Nancy, and Sally, and Prudy and Sue,
And a vast many others that none could outdo.

191

The sloop she was launched and got underway,
But Uncle soon found that the bitch would mis-stay.

So he put up the helm to wear her around,
But when she jibed over she struck hard ground.

And Uncle Josiah was all in a fret,
For fear he'd got taken in old Neptune's net.

Then Uncle Josiah says he to Sam,
"For a thousand such sloops I'd not give a damn."

But he called all hands to man the boat,
To take out an anchor and heave her afloat.

But Uncle Josiah did swamp it and swore
That he wished the darn vessel had rotted ashore.

They hove the boat off and they hoisted her sail
The wind all the time blew a powerful gale.

But they got her into the harbor snug,
And moored her safe as a bug in a rug.

And Uncle Josiah then scrambled ashore,
And swore that he'd never build sloops anymore.

THE NANTUCKET SKIPPER

J. T. Fields

Many a long, long year ago,
    Nantucket skippers had a plan
Of finding out, though "lying low,"
    How near New York their schooners ran.

They greased the lead before it fell,
    And then by sounding through the night,

The Nantucket Skipper

Knowing the soil that stuck so well
    They always guessed their reckoning right.

A skipper gray, whose eyes were dim,
    Could tell by tasting, just the spot.
And so below he'd douse the glim,
    After, of course, his "something hot."

Snug in his berth, at eight o'clock
    This ancient skipper might be found,
No matter how his craft would rock,
    He slept, for skipper's naps are sound.

The watch on deck would now and then
    Run down and wake him, with the lead;
He'd up and taste, and tell the man
    How many miles they went ahead.

One night 'twas Jotham Marden's watch,
    A curious wag — the peddler's son;
And so he mused (the wanton wretch)
    "Tonight I'll have a grain of fun.

"We're all a set of stupid fools
    To think the skipper knows by tasting,
What ground he's on; Nantucket schools
    Don't teach such stuff, with all their basting."

And so he took the well-greased lead
    And rubbed it o'er a box of earth
That stood on deck, a parsnip bed;
    And then he sought the skipper's berth.

"Where are we now, sir? Please to taste."
    The skipper yawned, put out his tongue,
Opened his eyes in wondrous haste,
    And then upon the floor he sprung.

The skipper swore and tore his hair,
    Hauled on his boots and roared to Marden,
"Nantucket's sunk, and here we are,
    Right over old Marm Hackett's garden!"

THE FATE OF THE NANCY BELL

W. S. Gilbert

'Twas in the good ship *Nancy Bell*
    That we sailed to the Indian Sea,
And there on a reef we came to grief
    Which has often occurred to me.

And pretty nigh all the crew were drowned
    (There was seventy-six o' soul)
And only ten of the *Nancy's* men
    Said "here" to the muster roll.

There was me and the cook and the captain bold
    And the mate of the *Nancy* brig,
And the bo'sun tight, and a midshipmite,
    And the crew of the captain's gig.

For a month we'd neither wittles nor drink,
    'Til a-hungry we did feel;
So we drawed a lot, and accordin' shot
    The captain for our meal.

The next lot fell to the *Nancy's* mate,
    And a delicate dish he made;
Then our appetite with the midshipmite
    We seven survivors stayed.

And then we murdered the bo'sun tight,
    And he much resembled a pig;
Then we wittled free, did the cook and me,
    On the crew of the captain's gig.

Then only the cook and me was left,
　　And the delicate question, "Which
Of us two goes to the kettle?" arose,
　　And we argued it out as sich.

For I loved that cook as a brother, I did,
　　And the cook he worshipped me;
But we'd both be blowed if we'd either be stowed
　　In the other chap's hold, you see.

"I'll be eat if you dines of me," says Tom;
　　"Yes that," says I, "you'll be."
"I'm boiled if I die, my friend," quoth I;
　　And "Exactly so," quoth he.

Says he, "Dear James, to murder me
　　Were a foolish thing to do.
For don't you see that you can't cook me,
　　While I can — and will — cook you?"

So he boils the water and takes the salt
　　And the pepper in portions true,
(Which he never forgot) and some chopped shallot,
　　And some sage and parsley too.

"Come here," says he, with a proper pride,
　　Which his smiling features tell,
" 'Twill soothing be if I let you see
　　How extremely nice you'll smell."

And he stirred it round and round and round,
　　And he sniffed at the foaming froth;
When I ups with his heels and smother his squeals
　　In the scum of the boiling broth.

And I eat the cook in a week or less,
　　And, as I eating be

The last of his chops, why, I almost drops,
    For a wessel in sight I see.

And I never grieve and I never smile,
    And I never larf or play,
But I sit and croak, and a single joke
    I have — which is to say:

"Oh, I am the cook, and a captain bold,
    And the mate of the *Nancy* brig,
And a bo'sun tight, and a midshipmite,
    And the crew of the captain's gig.

THE BARBER SONG

Vineyard *Gazette*

There was a young bar–ber who lived in the cit –y, he

was a me–lo–di–ous sweet–scent–ed cuss. His hair it was cur–ly, his

heels doub–led joint–ed, He nev–er was known for to kick up a fuss.

There was a young barber who lived in the city
    He was a melodious sweet-scented cuss.
His hair it was curly, his heels double jointed,
    He never was known for to kick up a fuss.

You could see him each morning a-honing his razor
    The people would gather in crowds 'round his door,

The Barber Song

And each would exclaim as he slapped on the lather,
    Such a sweet-scented barber they ne'er saw before.

There was a young maid named Matilda O'Brien,
    A marshal was she in a kitchen close by;
Every morning she walked on her way to the market,
    And into the barber's she'd throw a sheep's eye.

The barber would watch 'til he saw her returning,
    And then to the door he quickly would come.
A box of pomade he would slip in her basket,
    And then drink her health in a pint of bay rum.

Now a young butcher boy by the name of Hans Schneider,
    He heard of the barber and jealous he grew;
He loaded a platter with kidneys and doughnuts
    And straight to the sweet-scented barber he flew.

The battle commenced and the slaughter was awful,
    With murder intent on each other did rush;
The barber soon got the best of the butcher
    And blew out his brains with a lathering brush.

Matilda O'Brien, when she heard of the slaughter,
    She made up her mind to commit suicide;
She swallowed three gallons of brandy and water
    And went in the cellar and laid down and died.

The barber went crazy and busted his business,
    His policy quit and his money let fly;
He dwindled and dwindled clean down to a shadow,
    And poisoned himself with a box of hair dye.

The words to this song were also sung to the chantey, *Blow the Man Down.*

THE LIVERPOOL GIRLS

CAPSTAN

David T. Bone

When I was a young-ster I sailed with the rest, On a

Liv-er-pool pack-et bound out to the west. We an-chored a day in the

har-bor of Cork, then put out to sea for th' port o' New York An' it's

Ho! Ho! Ho! bul-lies ho! th' Liv-er-pool gir-ils have got us in tow.

When I was a youngster I sailed with the rest,
On a Liverpool packet bound out to the west.
We anchored a day in the harbor of Cork,
Then put out to sea for the port o' New York.
An' it's ho! Ho! Ho! Bullies ho!
Th' Liverpool girls have got us in tow.

For thirty-two days we was hungry an' sore
Th' wind was agin us an' gales they did roar;
But at Battery Point we did anchor at last
Wit' th' jib boom rigged in an' th' canvas all fast.

Th' boardin' house masters was off in a trice,
An' shoutin' an' promisin' all that was nice;

198

An' one fat old crimp he got cotton to me
  An' said I was foolish t' follow th' sea.

Sez he, "There's a job as is waitin' for you,
  Wit' oshins of likker an' nothin' t' do,
Now what d'ye say, lad, will ye jump her too?"
  Sez I, "Ye old beggar I'm damned if I do!"

But th' best of intentions they never go far,
  After thirty-two days, at the door of a bar
I tossed off me likker, an' what d'ye think?
  Th' dirty old rascal had drugs in me drink.

Th' next I remember, I woke in the morn
  In a three skysail yarder boun' south roun' th' horn,
Wit' an ol' suit o' oilskins an' two pair o' sox,
  An' a florin o' bricks at th' foot o' me box.

JOHN, JOHN CROW

HAND OVER HAND

Barbadian negro chantey, unloading cargo.

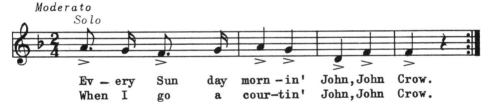

Moderato
Solo

Ev — ery   Sun   day   morn – in'   John, John   Crow.
When I   go   a   cour–tin'   John, John   Crow.

Every Sunday mornin',
  John, John Crow.
When I go a-courtin',
  John, John Crow.

Meet me in the sugar cane,
Dat is, if it doesn' rain.

Oh what kind of man is you?
Comin' 'round a-loafin' too.

Come down upon me lively,
Cut her nigger timely.

Good beefsteak and mutton chop,
Make yo' lips go flippety-flop.

Then I will drink my lime juice,
When I get in the calaboose.

Lawd, I went to my woman's do',
Jus' lak I bin goin' befo'.

"Come back 'bout half pas' fo',
If I'm done, I'll open de do'."

I keep rappin' on my woman's do',
Lak I never had been dere befo'.

"Nigger, you oughter do lak me:
Git a good woman and let me be."

GWINE TO GIT A HOME BIME BY
'BADIAN HAND OVER HAND

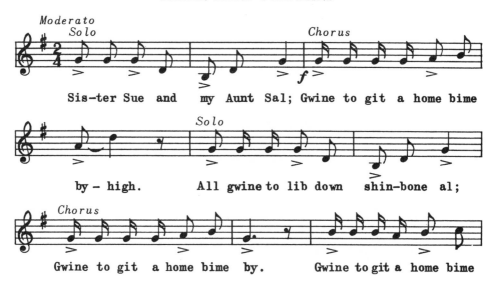

Sis-ter Sue and my Aunt Sal; Gwine to git a home bime by - high. All gwine to lib down shin-bone al; Gwine to git a home bime by. Gwine to git a home bime

by – e – high, gwine to git a home bime by.

Sister Sue and my Aunt Sal,
Gwine to git a home bime by-high.
All gwine to lib down shin-bone al;
Gwine to git a home bime by.
Gwine to git a home bime by-e-high,
Gwine to git a home bime by.

Dere ain't no use in my workin' so hard
For I got a gal in de white folks' yard.

She kill a chicken and bring me de wing;
Ain't I livin' on an easy thing?

Tole my cap'n my han's was cold;
"God damn yo' han's, let the ole ship roll!"

Oh, Cap'n Lamson is mighty damn mean,
I think he comes from New Orleans.

LINDY LOWE
'BADIAN HAND OVER HAND

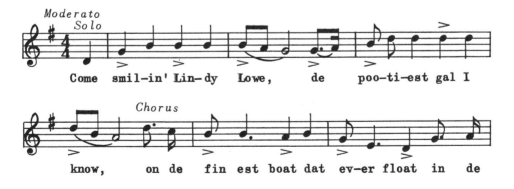

Come smil-in' Lin-dy Lowe, de poo-ti-est gal I

know, on de fin est boat dat ev-er float in de

O - hi - o, de Mis-sis-sip-pi or de O - hi - o.

Come smilin' Lindy Lowe,
De pootiest gal I know,
On de finest boat dat ever float
    In de Ohio,
De Mississippi or de Ohio.

Come smilin' Lindy Lowe,
To de Louisiana sho'.

Come smilin' Lindy Lowe,
By de Gulf ob Mexico.

Come smilin' Lindy Lowe,
To de bayous deep an' slow.

Come smilin' Lindy Lowe,
De bell done ring to go.

Come smilin' Lindy Lowe,
Befo' de whistle blow.

Come smilin' Lindy Lowe,
Git on board or row.

Come smilin' Lindy Lowe,
It'll cost yo' fifty cents.

Come smilin' Lindy Lowe,
'Cause yo' don't pay any rent.

THE DARKY SUNDAY SCHOOL
'BADIAN HAND OVER HAND

Andante
Solo

De earth was made in six days an' fin-ished on de

seventh. An''cord-in' to de con-tract, it should have been de

'lev-enth. De car-pen-ters got drunk an' de

ma-sons would-n't work, So de cheap-est thing to

Chorus

do was to fill it up wid dirt. Old folks,

young folks, ev-'ry-bod-y come. Join de dark-y

Sun-day School an' make yo'-se'f at home.

Leave yo' chunk ob chew-in' gum an'

ra-zor at de do', an' we'll tell yo' Bi-ble

sto-ries dat yo' neb-bah heard be-fo'.

De earth was made in six days an' finished on de seventh.
    An' 'cordin' to de contract, it should have been de 'leventh.
De carpenters got drunk an' de masons wouldn't work,
    So de cheapest thing to do was to fill it up wid dirt.

Old folks, young folks, ev'ry body come.
    Join de darky Sunday School an' make yo'se'f at home.
Leave yo' chunk ob chewin' gum an' razor at de do',
    An' we'll tell yo' Bible stories dat yo' nebbah heard befo'.

Adam was de fu'st man an' Eve she was his spouse,
    Dey lost their job ob swipin' fruit an' went to keepin' house;
All was berry peaceful an' quiet on de main,
    Until a little baby came an' dey started raisin' Cain.

De Lawd made de debbil an' de debbil made sin.
    De Lawd made a cubbyhole an' shoved de debbil in.
De debbil got sore an' said he wouldn't stay;
    De Lawd said he had to, 'cause he couldn't get away.

Noah was de keepah ob de Asiatic zoo,
    He built an ocean lina' when he hadn't much to do.
One day he got excited when de sky was gettin' dark,
    So he gathered all de animals an' put dem in de ark.

204

The Darky Sunday School

It rained fo' forty days an' it rained fo' forty nights.
  It rained so hard it washed de lan' completely out ob sight.
When Noah was a-wonderin' as to what he'd better do,
  De ark hit on Mt. Ararat an' stuck as tight as glue.

Abraham was a patriarch, de father ob his set.
  He took his little Ikey out to kill him on a bet.
An' he'd met his finish if it wasn't fo' a lamb,
  Fo' papa had his razor out an' didn't gib a damn.

Esau was a cowboy ob a wild and wooly make,
  His father gave him ha'f de lan' an' ha'f to brother Jake.
But when he saw de title to his lan' it wasn't clear,
  He sol' it to his brother fo' a sandwich an' a beer.

Daniel was a brave man who wouldn't mind de king,
  De king he said he nebbah once had heard ob such a thing.
He thrust him down a manhole wid lions all beneath,
  But Daniel was a dentist an' pulled de lions' teeth.

Jonah was an emigrant, so runs de Bible tale,
  He took an ocean voyage on a transatlantic whale.
But Jonah in de whale made de whale feel quite distressed,
  So Jonah pushed de button an' de whale soon did de rest.

David was a shepherd's boy, his mother's pride and joy.
  His father gave him a slingshot, a harmless little toy.
Along came Goliath a-lookin' fo' a fuss,
  So David heaved a cobblestone an' neatly caved his crust.

Sampson was a strong man ob John L. Sullivan's school.
  He killed a thousand Philistines wid de jaw bone ob a mule.
Along came a woman who filled him up wid gin,
  An' shaved off all his whiskers an' de coppers roped him in.

A chantey that was sung in the '60s but one I have never heard
was *Dixie's Isle*. A friend who made a voyage around the Horn, in
the ship *Young America*, said it was very popular there. The chorus

was the last line of each verse. There were more verses but the following were all that he could remember.

DIXIE'S ISLE

CAPSTAN

0, then Su - sie, love-ly Su - sie, I can no long-er stay. For the bu -gle sounds the warn - ing that calls me far a - way. It calls me down to New Or-leans, the en-e-my for to rile; And to fight the south-ern sol - diers 'way down on Dix-ie's Isle. And to fight the south-ern sol - diers 'way down on Dix - ie's Isle.

Dixie's Isle

O, then Susie, lovely Susie, I can no longer stay.
    For the bugle sounds the warning that calls me far away.
It calls me to New Orleans, the enemy for to rile;
    And to fight the southern soldiers 'way down on Dixie's Isle.
    And to fight the southern soldiers 'way down on Dixie's Isle.

The owners they gave orders no women were to come,
    The captain likewise ordered that none of them should come;
For their waists are much too slender and their figures not the style
    For to fight the southern soldiers 'way down on Dixie's Isle.

O, my curse attend those cruel wars and when first they began,
    They robbed New York and Boston of many a noble young man.
They robbed us of our sweethearts, our wives and brothers while
    We went fighting the southern soldiers 'way down on Dixie's Isle.

ABOARD THE HENRY CLAY

CAPSTAN

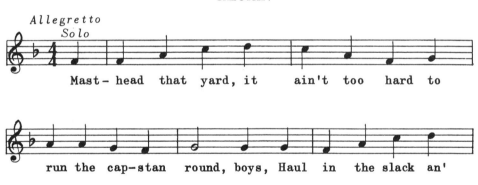

Mast-head that yard, it ain't too hard to

run the cap-stan round, boys, Haul in the slack an'

don't hang back, or the mate-'ll comb your

Chorus

hair, boys. Or the mate-'ll comb your hair, boys.

Masthead that yard, it ain't too hard
    To run the capstan round, boys,
Haul in the slack an' don't hang back,
    Or the mate'll comb your hair, boys.
    Or the mate'll comb your hair, boys.

Oh, make her spring and I will sing
    A chantey unto you, boys,
Of a lime-juice jay who has once too gay
    Aboard the *Henry Clay*, boys.

He was just to sea, with the Hook on our lee,
    Still crazy with the drink, boys,
An' the mate warn't riled when that half-baked child
    Went off into a fit, boys.

For he'd been on a tear an' warn't all there,
    But the mate he raised his boot, boys,
And lifted him slick with a hell of a kick
    Right off the fo'c'sle head, boys.

And that lime-juice jay went down to stay,
    He never cum up no more, boys,
But the mate didn't care, he'd got men to spare
    Aboard the *Henry Clay*, boys.

That night in the dark we found the mate stark
    With a knife in the small of his back, boys.
You say he's a blower and might ha' gone slower,
    But the mate was a joskin once, boys.

Hands at the windlass of the whaling bark *Charles W. Morgan*   (Mystic Seaport 1994.53.97)

Whaling Songs

IN 1868, JOHN Boyle O'Reilly, the Irish poet, was arrested with the Irish Fenians and imprisoned in Dartmoor, England, four months, then banished with others to Fremantel, Australia. He escaped the following year through friends who secured passage for him in the whaling bark *Gazelle*, Captain Gifford, of New Bedford, Massachusetts.

H. G. Hathaway, third mate of the bark, wrote a letter to a friend, from New Bedford in 1877, telling of an exciting encounter with a "bad whale" that turned on the whaleboat he and Mr. O'Reilly were in while off the northwest coast of Australia; reading in part:

"It was in May 1869, while lowering for whales, that Mr. O'Reilly asked to go with me in my boat. Reaching the whales, Mr. Hussey, in another boat, struck the first whale. He "settled" and the next thing I knew the whale's back was close to our boat. I told Lambert, the boatsteerer to 'give it to him!' As soon as we struck him the whale raised his flukes and struck our boat four successive times, knocking her to atoms. The crew jumped into the sea and clung to their oars. I clung to the stern part of the boat, that being the only piece left large enough to hold up a man. When the whale left us the men swam back to the shattered boat. I remember saying, "O! My God where is Mr. O'Reilly?" Bolter who was next to me close by, said, "There he is on the other side, under the water." There he was about two feet from the surface of the water bobbing up and down like a cork. I threw myself over and by clinging to the broken keel (which was about ten feet long) with my

210

left hand, I reached him by the hair of his head with my right hand and hauled him on the stoven boat, froth running from his mouth and nostrils. I raised him on my shoulder as I lay on the side of the boat, with his stomach across my shoulder. I kept punching to get the salt water out of him. It was several hours before he realized anything. In the meantime we were picked up by Mr. Bryan, the fourth mate.

"Several days later we again raised whales, and Mr. O'Reilly asked to go with me and said, 'I want to get revenge.'

"We were lucky enough that day to get a good big fellow and I think O'Reilly got his revenge, as we minced him up pretty well. I think it was the death of that whale that suggested his poem *The Amber Whale*."

When the whale is alongside and the great dripping blanket-piece is being cut in, every pound of which represents so much gold, the sweating, oil-soaked, greasy crew would burst into some such song as:

> My father's a hedger and ditcher.
> My mother does nothing but spin,
> While I hunt whales for a living.
> Good Lord how the money comes in.

IT'S ADVERTISED IN BOSTON
WINDLASS

Oh, it's ad-ver-tised in Bos-ton, New York and Buf-fa-lo, One

hun-dred men are want-ed a - whal-ing for to go.

211

Cheer up my live-ly lads in spite of wind-y wea-ther,

Cheer up my live-ly lads we'll all get drunk to-ge-ther.

Oh, it's advertised in Boston, New York and Buffalo,
One hundred men are wanted, a-whaling for to go.

Cheer up my lively lads, in spite of stormy weather,
Cheer up my lively lads, we'll all get drunk together.

They'll take you to New Bedford, they'll ship you off to sea
And charge you sixty dollars for two suits of dungaree.

They'll send you to a boarding house and for a time to dwell,
The thieves are thicker there than on the other side of hell.

You're put aboard some staunch old bark, so able, trim, and stout,
And told that you will get her full before you're six months out.

They'll show you all the running gear and that you've got to know,
If you don't learn in a week, you'll lose your watch below.

Then comes the bloody compass, that grieves us all quite sore,
It has but two and thirty points. You'll swear there's sixty-four.

You'll go down to your dinner next, and find not half enough,
It's of a nasty piece of junk, besides some claggy duff.

And now we're out to sea my boys, the wind begins to blow,
Some are sick as hell on deck, the rest are down below.

You'll try to pass the galley with one eye up on the mate,
You'll smell the "old horse" cooking there, when up comes all you've ate.

He'll drag you to the topmast head, where you'll ride out the gale,
He'll promise you ten dollars there, if you can raise a whale.

Then, when you raise a whale, "she bl-o-w-s!" you heartily do cry,
The ten dollars that you were to get is something in your eye.

But now, you have him killed, my boy, and towed him alongside,
The next thing we will have to do, is rob him of his hide.

The boat steerer is over side to clear and overhaul,
The Old Man's in the main channels and loudly he does bawl.

The cooper at his workbench now, is making iron poles,
The mate upon the main hatch stands, a-cursing all our souls.

The whale cut up, tried out, the oil below is stowed away,
There's fifty cents a-coming to the hundred fifteenth lay.

Then, when the decks are all cleaned up and we're all neat and dry,
Your ten dollars you'll get — of course — when pigs begin to fly.

'TWAS A LOVE OF ADVENTURE

'Twas a love of adventure and a longing for gold
    And a hardened desire to roam,
Tempted me far away o'er the watery world,
    Far away from my kindred and home.

With a stern-beaten captain so fearless and bold
    And a score of brave fellows or two,
Far away to the hardships, the hunger and cold,
    Sailed this fearless and jovial crew.

Have you ever cruised on Diego's bold shores,
    That are washed by the Antarctic wave,
Where the white-plumed albatross merrily soars
    O'er many a poor sailor's grave?

213

Did you ever hear tell of that mighty sperm whale,
    That when boldly attacked in his lair,
With one sweep of his mighty and ponderous tail
    Sends the whaleboat so high in the air?

Did you ever join in with those heat ringing cheers
    With your face turned to heaven's blue dome,
As laden with riches you purchased so dear,
    You hoisted your topsails, bound home?

A HOME ON THE MOUNTAIN WAVE

A bold, brave crew and an o - cean blue, and a
ship that loves the blast, And a good wind pi -ping
mer - ri - ly in the tall and gal - lant
mast. Ha ha, my boys, these are the joys of the
no - ble and the brave, Who love the life in the
tem-pest's strife and a home on the moun - tain wave.

A Home on the Mountain Wave

A bold, brave crew and an ocean blue,
    And a ship that loves the blast,
And a good wind piping merrily
    In the tall and gallant mast.

Ha, ha, my boys, these are the joys
    Of the noble and the brave,
Who love the life in the tempest's strife
    And a home on the mountain wave.

When the driving rain of the hurricane
    Puts the gleam of the lighthouse out,
And the growling thunder sounds its gong
    Of the whirlwind's battle route.

Ha, ha, do you think that the valiant shrink?
    No, no! We are bold and brave!
And we love to fight, in the wild midnight,
    With the storm on the mountain wave.

Breezes that die where the green woods sigh,
    To the landsman sweet may be,
But give to the brave the broad-backed wave
    And the tempest's midnight glee!

Ha, ha, the blast, and the rocking mast,
    And the sea wind brisk and cold,
And thunder's jar, on the seas afar,
    Are the things that suit the bold.

The timbers creak, the sea birds shriek;
    There's lightening in yon blast!
Hard to the leeward, mariners,
    For the storm is gathering fast!

Ha, ha, tonight, boys, we must fight,
    But the winds, which o'er us yell,

Shall never scare the mariner
In his winged citadel.

The above "old timer" was sung in New Bedford by my father
and brothers before I was born, or before any of us went to sea. I have
never seen the music, but give it as my brother Wiley sang it.

OLD NANTUCKET WHALING SONG

Oh, come all ye brave mariners
Who plow the raging main.
Who go to sea in leaky ships
And safe return again.
Come listen to my story

216

Old Nantucket Whaling Song

That I will now relate,
Concerning our brave whaling men
And their most dismal fate.

'Tis first we work six months or so
Our ship to fit away,
Then to Nantucket bar we go
And there in prison lay,
Until the day it does come round
That we may all set sail,
We're bound unto the Southern Sea
And there to cruise for whale.

'Tis then we cross the Atlantic
Six thousand miles or so,
'Til we arrive off that dread cape
Where stormy winds do blow.
'Tis here we'll be a month perhaps,
Just as the fates agree,
All at the mercy of the winds
And of the raging sea.

But if at length we weather it,
In spite of gales of wind,
Then on the coast of Chile
Cold rain and storms we'll find,
Which makes us wear our jackets,
And blow our fingers sore,
And wish full often, where we've been,
That we might be once more.

'Tis there we'll cruise a month or two
And never see a whale.
Our water all stagnated grows,
And our provisions fail.
Dull prospects all around us
While our good ship onward goes.

At last, from our masthead, a cry,
    "Oh, there, oh, there she blows!"

"Oh, where away?" our captain cries,
    Then quickly runs aloft.
"Three points off our weather bow
    And scarcely two miles off."
'Tis then we jump with glee
    To clear the boats away
We soon were on the ocean blue
    All fitted for the fray.

The mate who takes the steering oar
    As o'er the sea we fly,
He cries, "There lies a large sperm whale
    A-spouting towards the sky.
Now pull away! And bend your oars!
    We'll single out that bull.
Now give away! And bend your backs.
    Come, altogether, pull!"

Now, when at length you reach the whale,
    Upon your oars you lay;
"All ready forward, heave your iron!
    G-d d--n it, heave, I say!"
The bold harpooner stands erect
    And heaves with all his strength;
The iron darts true to his aim
    And buries half its length.

"We're fast! Starn all! Get out of his way,
    And give his flukes more room."
And out from under that mountain of flesh
    Your boat's backed none too soon.
With mighty plunge head-first below,
    The water he'll displace

Will send a whirling, seething foam
    To splash you in the face.

When forty fathoms of your line
    Runs out, you take a turn
Around the loggerhead it runs
    And smoking seems to burn.
"Wet line! Wet line!" is now the cry.
    And next, "She's running slack!
Haul in, my boys, together haul!
    And keep upon his track!"

The monster then comes up to spout.
    New danger will you know;
If he shows no fight, he'll turn in flight
    And straight to windward go.
'Twill be the fastest sail you've had
    And something new to you;
And when you meet the rising waves
    You'll cut them through and through.

Your boat goes through each wave until
    Your gunwale's down below,
And the water raises far above,
    A foot or more you know.
You'll haul in the whale, my boy,
    To thrust a lance within;
But he'll give you all the fun you want
    Before out runs his fin.

EDGARTOWN WHALING SONG[1]

Tune: *Old Nantucket Whaling Song*

Come all ye girls of Edgartown,
    A line to you I'll write,
While crossing o'er the ocean wide
    In which we take delight,

In sailing o'er these raging seas
    As we poor sailors do,
Not like those lazy landlubbers
    Who stay at home with you.

They'll stay at home with you, my dears,
    And tell with lips unsealed,
Concerning all their harvest work
    That's done in our corn fields,
In cutting off the grass so green,
    It's all that they can do;
While we like jovial hearted lads,
    Go plow the ocean through.

We plow the ocean through, my dears,
    And smell the salt sea breeze;
We haven't any barnyard smell
    About our dungarees.
Our necks and arms are sunburnt brown
    From tropic seas we bring,
As jolly a set of sailor lads
    That ever yards did swing.

We cruised about the Southern Seas
    For sperm and humps as well,
And many a whale we fastened to;
    We've got a yarn to tell.
In fourteen months we filled the ship
    And then the welcome sound
Of "Square away, and make all sail,"
    For we are homeward bound.

We crossed the line in thirty-five
    And struck the nothe-east trades
In latitude something like eight,
    Before the evening shades.
Then, all went well with all sails set

220

Edgartown Whaling Song

'Til Hatteras on our lee,
The wind backed round to nor-nor-west
    And kicked up an awful sea.

A circle round the moon is seen,
    The wind begins to blow;
"All hands on deck!" the captain cries,
    "All hands from down below!"
All hands from down below, brave boys,
    Our goodly ship he guards,
"Jump up aloft! Damn lively, lads!
    Send down topgallant yards!"

'Twas lower away, and shorten sail
    And up the rigging bound
For royal and topgallant yards
    We soon had lowered down.
We had the yards soon down on deck,
    And ran before the gale,
Because the wind kept backing round,
    As we were shortening sail.

Three days we drove her though the sea
    And under bare poles we sailed,
With lightning flashes from above,
    At times it rained and hailed.
We ran before the hurricane,
    As east the wind did draw,
While six points off the lee port bow
    Nantucket Isle we saw.

The wind did from the nothe-east blow
    It tossed us up and down;
And scudding past Monomoy Point
    Into Nantucket Sound.
Our captain cries, "Hurrah, my boys,
    We plow the raging main.

We'll soon drop anchor in Edgartown
And see those girls again."

Now, into Oldtown* harbor
Our gallant ship we steer,
And every heart with vigor beats
To think of friends so dear.
Tonight around our flowing bowl
We'll drive dull care away,
And toast each blooming pretty lass
In dear America.

*Edgartown

THE COAST OF PERU

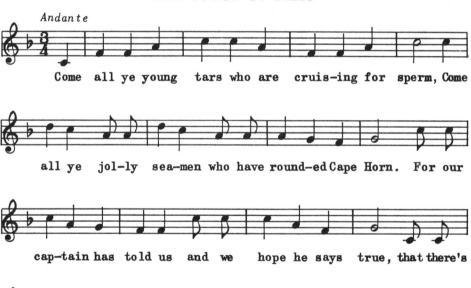

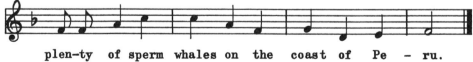

Come all ye young tars who are cruising for sperm,
Come all ye jolly seamen who have rounded Cape Horn:
For our captain has told us and we hope he says true,
That there's plenty of sperm whales on the coast of Peru.

The first whale we saw near the close of the day.
    Our captain came on deck and thus he did say:
"Now, all my good sailors, pray be of good glee,
    For we'll see him in the mornin' p'rhaps under our lee."

It was early next morning, just as the sun 'rose,
    The man at the masthead cried out, "'Ere she blows!"
"Where away?" cried our captain, as he sprang aloft,
    "Three points off our lee beam and scarce two miles off."

"Now brace up your yards, boys, and be of good cheer,
    Get your lines in your boats, see your box lines all clear;
Haul back the main yard, boys, stand by, each boat crew,
    Lower away, lower away! when the main yard swings to!

"Now bend to your oars, boys, just make the boat fly.
    But whatever you do, boys, keep clear from his eye."
The first mate soon struck and the whale he went down,
    While the Old Man pulled up and stood by to bend on.

But the whale soon arose, to the windward, he lay,
    We hauled up 'longside, and he showed us fair play.
We caused him to vomit thick blood for to spout,
    And in less than ten minutes we rolled him "fin out."

We towed him alongside with many a shout,
    That day, cut him in and begin to boil out.
Oh, now he's all boiled out and stowed down below,
    We're waiting to hear 'em sing out, "'Ere she blows!"

THE WHALE[2]

Capt. W. B. Whall

Oh, 'twas in the year of nine-ty-four, and of

June the sec-ond day, That our gal-lant ship her

an - chor weighed, and from Strom-ness bore a -

Chorus

way, brave boys, And from Strom-ness bore a - way.

Oh, 'twas in the year of ninety-four,
 And of June the second day,
That our gallant ship her anchor weighed,
 And from Stromness bore away, brave boys,
 And from Stromness bore away.

Now Speedicut was our captain's name,
 And our ship the *Lion* bold,
And we were bound to far Greenland,
 To the land of ice and cold, brave boys,
 To the land of ice and cold.

And when we came to far Greenland,
 And to Greenland cold we came,
Where there's ice, and there's snow, and the whalefishes blow,
 We found all open sea, brave boys,
 We found all open sea.

Then the mate he climbed to the crow's nest high,
 With his spyglass in his hand,
"There's a whale, there's a whale, there's a whalefish!" he cried,
 "And she blows at every span," brave boys,
 And she blows at every span.

224

The Whale

Our captain stood on his quarterdeck,
    And a fine little man was he,
"Overhaul, overhaul, on your davit tackle fall,
    And launch your boats to the sea," brave boys,
    And launch your boats to the sea.

Now the boats were launched and the men aboard,
    With the whalefish full in view,
Resolved were the whole boat's crew
    To steer where the whalefish blew, brave boys,
    To steer where the whalefish blew.

And when we reached that whale, my boys,
    He lashed out with his tail,
And we lost a boat and seven good men
    And we never caught that whale, brave boys,
    And we never caught that whale.

Bad news, bad news to our captain came,
    That grieved him very sore,
But when he found that his cabin boy was gone,
    Why it grieved him ten times more, brave boys,
    Why it grieved him ten times more.

Oh, Greenland is an awful place,
    Where the daylight's seldom seen.
Where there's ice and snow, where the whalefishes blow.
    Then adieu to cold Greenland, brave boys,
    Then adieu to cold Greenland.

THE GREENLAND WHALE[3]
CAPSTAN

In eight-een hun-dred and for-ty-nine on the

225

fif-teenth day of   May,   we   raised our an—chor and

Chorus

set   our   sails,   and   for   Green—land sailed a —

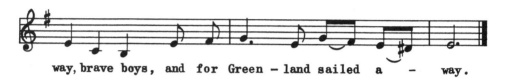

way, brave boys, and for Green — land sailed a — way.

In eighteen hundred and forty-nine
　　On the fifteenth day of May,
We raised our anchor and set our sails,
　　And for Greenland sailed away, brave boys,
　　And for Greenland sailed away.

The captain's name was William Moore,
　　And the mate was Mister Lane;
The ship was called the *Lioness,*
　　And she sailed the boundless main, brave boys,
　　And she sailed the boundless main.

The captain stood on the quarterdeck
　　With a spyglass in his hand;
"A whale! A whale! A whale!" cried he;
　　"There she blows! A devil of a strand," brave boys,
　　There she blows a devil of a strand!

The mate, he stood on the forward deck
　　And a nice young man was he;
"Lower away! Lower away on your davit tackle falls
　　And launch your boats to the sea," brave boys,
　　And launch your boats to the sea.

226

The Greenland Whale

In the captain's boat were five jolly tars
    And our little cabin boy, full of pride;
And they gave three cheers as they pulled for the whale
    And they soon had an iron in her side, brave boys,
    And they soon had an iron in her side.

"Stern all! Stern all!" was the boat steerer's cry,
    When she gave a sudden flurry with her tail;
And over went the boat with the five jolly tars
    And to Davy Jones' locker did they sail, brave boys,
    And to Davy Jones' locker did they sail.

When the captain heard of the loss of his crew,
    It grieved his heart very sore;
But when he heard of the death of his little cabin boy,
    It grieved his ten times more, brave boys,
    It grieved him ten times more.

THE HORN OF THE HIRAM Q

L. E. Richards

The *Hiram Q* was a whaler bold
    That sailed the roaring sea;
She'd a right smart skipper and an all sorts crew,
    And the wust of them all was old fool you,
And the best of them all was me.

With a yo, ho, and there she blows;
    Steer for her tail and you'll fetch her nose,
With a la-de-da, and a how d'ye do,
    And hark for the horn of the Hiram Q.

We was cruisin' down the Grinlan' coast,
    Where the skipper he says, says he,
"My boys, it feels like a whale, I snum,
    Just peel your eyes and look out some,
And the man that sights her first, by gum—"
    And the name of that man was me.

We was snoopin' down on the Grinlan' coast,
    When the cachalot hove in view,
And the biggest fool that ever was born,
    He fetched a toot on the *Hiram*'s horn
By gorry, you'd think 'twas the judgment horn,
    And the name of that fool was you.

When I see them whale on the Grinlan' coast,
    There was all the fam-i-lee.
But the old bull he says to the cow,
    "D'ye hear that noise on the weather bow?
It's git up and git or there'll be a row,
    For here comes the *Hiram Q*, I swow,"
And the hull of them put to sea.

ROLLING DOWN TO OLD MAUI[4]

'Tis now we're bound from the Arc-tic grounds. A-bound-ing o'er the main. And soon the hills of the trop-ic isles our eyes shall greet a - gain. Sev-en long moons have waxed and waned since last from port sailed

Rolling Down to Old Maui

we. But now we're bound from the Arc-tic ground, Rol-ling

Chorus

down to old Ma - ui. Rol-ling down to old Ma -

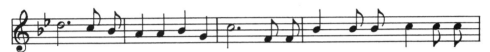

ui, rol-ling down to old Ma - ui. With our old bag-gy sails spread be-

fore the Arc-tic gales, rol-ling down to old Ma - ui.

'Tis now we're bound from the Arctic grounds.
    A-bounding o'er the main.
And soon the hills of the tropic isles
    Our eyes shall greet again.
Seven long moons have waxed and waned
    Since last from port sailed we.
But now we're bound for the Arctic ground,
    Rolling down to old Maui.*

Rolling down to old Maui,
    Rolling down to old Maui.
With our baggy sails spread before the Arctic gales,
    Rolling down to old Maui.

These northern gales they do blow strong,
    O'er East Cape well away,
That swept through the mist by the moonbeams kissed
    O'er the broad St. Lawrence Bay.
The hoary piles of shoals and isles
    That deck the arctic sea;

*Pronounced "Mo-hee."

'Tis many and many we've left astern,
    Rolling down to old Maui.

We'll heave our lead where old Diamond Head
    Looms up on old Oahu,
With our sails and rigging all covered with ice
    And white our decks below;
With a freshening gale on our port beam,
    And breakers on our lee,
As the bristling wind comes whistling past
    Sent tidings to old Maui.

'Tis a fearful life of strife and care,
    We whalemen undergo,
But what care we when the storm is o'er
    How hard the blast did blow?
We're homeward bound, 'tis a joyful sound,
    With a full ship, tight and free.
We'll not care for that, as we laugh and chat
    With the girls of old Maui.

BAFFIN'S BAY

Tune: *The Yankee Man of War*   As sung by Fred Stone

'Twas on the good ship *Cuspidore,*
    We sailed for Baffin's Bay;
We tied her to the ocean while
    The bullwarks ate some hay.
The captain said, "We'll tie the ship
    Whatever else betide;"
Then he drank a quart of gasoline
    With whiskey on the side.
He had lost his breath but soon it was restored.

Avast! Belay!
    We're off for Baffin's Bay.
We couldn't find the pole because

Baffin's Bay

The barber'd moved away;
The ship grew cold,
  We thought it had the grip,
So the painter put three coats upon
  The ship, hip, hip
Hooray! for Baffin's Bay.

Two friendly whales got in our net,
  We saw they were insane,
When one began to blubber,
  He had water on the brain.
The bull whale said, "Soapine,
  I love you best of all the whales."
Soapine said, "Hush, don't talk so loud,
  The fishes carry tails."
So the bull whale kissed her with a fishing smack.

It was midnight on the ocean,
  It was one beside the dock,
But by the larboard watch 'twas only
  Half past nine o'clock.
The captain said, "Unhitch the mules,
  We're going through the lock."
So the bo'sun took the starboard watch
  And put it right in hock,
'Cause the good ship didn't have a cent a board.

THE WHALEMEN'S WIVES

Capt. R. W. Nye

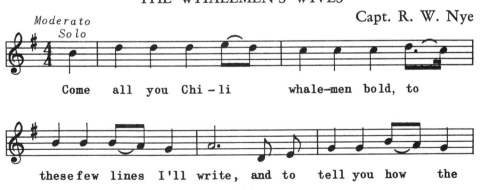

Moderato
Solo

Come all you Chi-li whale-men bold, to
these few lines I'll write, and to tell you how the

Come all you Chili whalemen bold,
  To these few lines I'll write,
And to tell you how the game goes on
  When you are out of sight.
Just to let you know how the lads on shore
  Go sporting with your wives,
While you are on the raging deep
  Endangering your sweet lives.
While you are on the raging deep
  Endangering your sweet lives.

232

The Whalemen's Wives

Our goodly ship she's outward bound,
    It is her sailing day.
"May the Lord above protect my love
    When he is far away.
And steer him clear of rocks and shoals,
    Never more will he return,
Until his pockets are well lined,
    And then he's welcome home."
Until his pockets are well lined,
    And then he's welcome home.

Then away she goes to the Flaya Ancha
    For a last fond look and sigh;
Her handkerchief from her pocket takes
    And wipes her tearless eye.
"My husband dear has gone to sea.
    Oh, sad it is, my case.
But there's plenty more upon the shore,
    Another must take his place."
But there's plenty more upon the shore,
    Another must take his place.

Then away she runs to her fancy man,
    And unto him doth say,
"My husband, he has gone to sea
    And tomorrow's his half-pay day.
If you'll wait for me by the office door
    Until I do come out,
This very day we'll sweat his pay
    And drink both ale and stout."
This very day we'll sweat his pay
    And drink both ale and stout.

The half-pay it's all gone and spent
    And the money is no more.
Said she, "My dear, be of good cheer,

233

The old man's far from shore,
Perhaps he's at the t'gallant masthead
    A-shivering with the cold,
Or perhaps he's fast to a bull humpback
    'Way down on Suar Shoal.
Or perhaps he's fast to a bull humpback
    'Way down on Suar Shoal.

Our goodly ship, she's home at last
    And anchored in the bay.
"I hear the news, my husband's come;
    To him I must away!"
Then away she runs to her neighbor's house,
    Saying, "One thing of you I want,
Lend me your gown for mine's in pawn,
    It's the only one I've got."
Lend me your gown for mine's in pawn,
    It's the only one I've got.

WHILE I'M AT THE WHEEL

THE "southerly buster" which the *Akbar* encountered while coal
laden from Newcastle, Australia, for Java caused her to alter course
to put into the port of Sydney for repairs. Gales from all points of
the compass blew with hurricane force but, leaking badly, she reached
Sydney after thirty days of extreme heavy weather.

Ship of the Seas, with glittering spars,
  Your mainsail is reefed by eleven Jack tars;
Light sails are furled, but no man's at rest
  It looks like a gale or high wind, at best;
I raise my eyes to look at the sky
  Where winds from the north roll waves mountains high;
Over the rail, seas green do reveal,
  A nasty head sea, and I'm at the wheel.

Ship of the Seas, a song as we go;
  The main sheet's hauled aft to *Haul away Joe!*
"Luff's" the command, 'twill ease up the sail,
  But watch for a comber to slop o'er the rail;
Into the wind, now, dip in your nose,
  We'll have a wet deck as everyone knows.
Haul away, Joe! comes peal after peal;
  A sea sweeps the deck, but I'm at the wheel.

Ship of the Seas, now shake yourself clear;
  The men are wet through, yet sing with a cheer;
Akbar old ship, rise up on your toe
  And clear the next sea as onward we go.
You'd like to run o'er the seas we just passed,
  You can't get away for I hold you fast;
Kick as you will, your tiller of steel,
  Will hold you, "old girl," for I'm at the wheel.

Ship of the Seas, the mate cries "Belay!"
  The old man growls out, "Keep full, don't delay!"
Up goes the helm — "Keep full, sir!" say I,
  Away goes the ship on a course, "Full and by!"

At the wheel of the bark *Alice* (Mystic Seaport 1996.113.1.85)

WHILE I'M AT THE WHEEL

With everything well for an hour or two
 The seas running high, the gale stronger blew;
The ship in a strain, I work in my zeal
 To keep near the wind, while I'm at the wheel.

Ship of the Seas, a command in a roar,
 "Lower away with your topsails; both mizzen and fore!"
Away up the rigging those jolly tars ran,
 To hand the big topsails that took every man;
High are the seas, now watch her my lad,
 That green sea ahead looks angry and mad.
Lord! what a plunge. You shook to your keel
 And buried yourself, but I'm at the wheel.

Ship of the Seas, it came in a flop
 And drenched the men through up in the fore top.
Galley doors gone and seas through them flow
 To rob the poor cook of his sleep down below;
Akbar old ship, you stagger and shake.
 Your foremast is sprung as seas o'er us break.
Backropes and guys are gone and you reel.
 Spare boats are stove in, but I'm at the wheel.

Ship of the Seas, the gale's like a thief
 It stripped you of jibs and spanker we'll reef
We clewed up the mainsail and took in the sail,
 Now everything's snug and we'll ride out the gale.
The sailors came down from aloft in a row
 And cleaned up the decks and the watch sent below;
Sounding the pumps it seemed most unreal,
 Six inches we've made while I'm at the wheel.

Ship of the Seas, new orders I hear,
 'Tis "Wear ship for Sydney. Port Jackson Heads, steer!"
Fierce is the gale; and the wind, nothing new,
 Shrieks through the rigging as we are "hove to."
Rip! goes a sail.   It's 'nough to lose heart;
 The main topsail sheet to windward doth part.

Strongest the gale in this last ordeal,
    And loud are the oaths while I'm at the wheel.

Ship of the Seas, hark — out of the din —
    "Goose-wing the topsail. We won't take it in;
Lay aloft lively! the weather clew save!"
    Our captain he shouts with face very grave.
Grasping the shrouds, those jolly Jack tars,
    All running aloft, lay out on the spars;
Gaskets are passed; it's so nice to feel,
    That everything's snug, while I'm at the wheel.

Ship of the Seas, with seas going down,
    We'll head her for Sydney and turn the ship 'round.
"Up hel'um's" the order, 'twill swing off the bow;
    "Spanker, haul down, with a man or two, now!
Square in the yards of the mizzen's" the cry,
    And "Follow it up with the main!" standing by;
Now, we're "before it" in a ver'table weel.
    We're safe from all danger, and I'm at the wheel.

Ship of the Seas, we'll pump you today
    With chantey you've heard, *A Fal-de-lal-day.*
Whistling songs, old sailors dislike,
    But started this one in dead of the night.
Take warning boys, old Jack's there to tell
    By singing this chantey, we'll all go to h--l;
For, whistling on ships our lips we must seal
    Or consequence take; but I'm at the wheel.

Ship of the Seas, the old shellbacks "bucked",
    And "laid off" the chantey before the pumps sucked;
Changing the watch in the morning I hear,
    "We'll splice the main brace with a bottle of cheer."
The steward then brought out a bottle of gin,
    And all hands came aft with a smile and a grin.
"Here's to the ship! Our captain we kneel.
    We'll drink to his health." But — I'm at the wheel.

F. P. Harlow

A NOTE ON SAILOR ETIQUETTE

I HAVE tried to explain the chanties and sing outs that are peculiar to the sailor. In this connection I might add that the sailor in '70's took great pride in sailor etiquette. I was the youngest of four brothers, all deepwater sailors, who took particular pains to tell me that everything aboard ship follows the sun. The sun rose in the east to the left, and set in the west to the right. Therefore one must coil a rope from left to right. The tiller ropes, lanyards, watch tackles, etc., must follow in this order. In mooring ship, one runs a line ashore and around a cleat or pile from left to right, and coming inboard takes a turn around the capstan in the same manner.

The points in the mariner's compass run from north to south in the eastward, and I was told in boxing the compass to draw an imaginary line from north to south, separating the compass into two halves.

The sailor's etiquette is vastly different from the landsman's. He took the liberty to change the points, north and south, into two different pronunciations, calling north *nothe* and south *southe,* thus making a soft sound for all points east and a hard sound for points west. And so we have the cardinal points for the sailor pronounced as follows:

The soft sound for points east	*The hard sound for points west*
Nothe	Southe
Nothe by east	Sou' by west
No'-nothe-east	Sou'-sou'-west
Nothe-east by nothe	Sou'-west by sou'
Nothe-east	Sou'-west
Nothe-east by east	Sou'-west by west
East-nothe-east	West-sou'-west
East by nothe	West by sou'
East	West
East by southe	West by nor'
East-southe-east	West-nor'-west
Southe-east by east	Nor'-west by west

Southe-east	Nor'-west
Southe-east by southe	Nor'-west by nor'
Sou'-southe-east	Nor'-nor'-west
Southe by east	Nor' by west

Many sailors of today disregard the hard and soft sounds, showing that times and customs change as we grow older. I have heard many a sailor — even pilots on Puget Sound — say, "The wind was nor'-east," which is enough to put a crimp in one's tongue. But it may be wrong for me to criticise.

Joanna C. Colcord in her *Sea Language Comes Ashore* gives us to understand the sailor's pronunciation of different points of the compass in her time at sea in her father's vessels, 50 years later than when I was a sailor, as: Nor'-nuth'-east; *southe* by west; west by *nothe*; nor'-west by *nothe* and *nothe* by west." Her *surge* is "To let the capstan run back a pawl or two." This is evidently a modern capstan, not one that I have been "shipmates" with. She defines a booby hatch as "Leading to storage space under the poop deck." The *Akbar* carried her booby hatch on the main deck, covering the mizzen hatch, and the hatch leading to storage space on the poop we called the "lazarette." How times do change.

Another expression heard these days that is fierce! "He walked the wind'ard side of the poop," or again, "The lu'ard side." He might as well say "Him and her done it." In my day it was the weather and lee side, for one must walk to wind'ard to gain the weather side, and walk to lu'ard to be on the lee side.

FOOTNOTES

CHANTEYING ON THE AKBAR

[1]Joanna C. Colcord, in her *Roll and Go,* mentions this chantey giving the words to the chorus as, "Clear *away* the track, let the bulgine run." Her footnote reads:

> Sharp says that the air is a variant of the Irish folk song *Shule Agra* and the "low-back car" would support this origin. The probability is that some Irish sailor, ashore on liberty in Mobile, sang *Shule Agra* in a waterfront saloon. It pleased the negroes hanging about outside and the next day they sang what they could remember while screwing cotton in some Liverpool ship's hold.

Wherever it originated, there is no doubt that the negroes twisted the words to suit themselves after hearing it sung, whether from *Shule Agra* or not. It was bad enough at that and unless different words were sung from those we used, I doubt she ever heard a ship's crew sing the chantey, because, being a woman, no chanteyman would dare to sing the words where she could hear them and, if started, the officer of the deck would bring him up sharply with a "round turn."

[2]Laura A. Smith, an English writer, mentions this chantey in her *Music of the Waters.* Her music and words are quite different from those we sang.

[3]*Hanging Johnny* is mentioned in Joanna C. Colcord's *Roll and Go,* where she quotes John Masefield as follows:

> It has a melancholy tune that is one of the saddest things I have ever heard. I heard it for the first time off the Horn, in a snowstorm, when we were hoisting topsails after heavy weather. There was a heavy gray sea running, and the decks were awash. The skys were sodden and oily, shutting in the sea about a quarter of a mile away. Some birds were flying about us, scream-ing. I thought at the time that it was the whole thing set to music. I cannot repeat those words to their melancholy, wavering music without seeing the line of yellow oilskins, the wet deck, the frozen ropes, and the great gray seas running up into the sky.

It is to be regretted that Miss Colcord wrote this rousing chantey in 4/4 time, making a monologue of the song, as it were, and only befitting old sailors with lame backs and one foot in the tarpaulin ready to be sewed up and launched overboard.

A hoisting chanty must have a swing and a sway to fit the activities of the sailors, who throw their whole weight from their shoulders, oscillating from side to side while hoisting at the fall.

In 1878 I made a voyage to Barbados in the bark *Conquest* of Boston. The negro stevedores at the fall where the cargo was hoisted by hand, sang this chantey day after day, using words for all relations, including hanging the baby as well as the bull pup, the pigs and the goats. The harmony of their voices outshone any college quartet ever heard. It was a standoff between *Hanging Johnny* and *I Love the Blue Mountains of Tennessee* as to which they liked best.

It was in the month of June and those negroes worked in the hot sun, singing away as they worked, until the leading chanteyman was out of breath, only to be relieved by another nearly his equal. Such singing I never expect to hear again under similar circumstances.

As John Masefield recalls the deck scene off Cape Horn, I recall a deck scene under a tropical sun at Bridgetown, Barbados, where worked four negroes at the fall,

241

their faces shining from perspiration that stood out like silvery beads against their black skin.

The leading chanteyman wore a red bandana handkerchief tied loosely around his neck and flowing over his shoulders partly covered with a dungaree jumper which was unbuttoned at the throat, exposing his black skin devoid of underclothing and shining like polished ebony. The whites of his eyes shone brightly as he pulled at the fall and the whipcords in his neck stood out like a pair of swifters showing the strain he was under as he sang hour after hour. He improvised words as only a negro poet could, at times so comical as to cause his companions to laugh heartily when forced to use too many words in the metre to make up the rhyme. They were a happy lot and good stevedores so long as they chanteyed. But without the chantey they were too lazy to get out of their own way.

[4]Richard H. Dana in his *Two Years Before the Mast* says, "There is a story current among seamen that a beef dealer was convicted, at Boston, of having sold old horses for ship's stores, instead of beef, and had been sentenced to be confined in jail until he should eat the whole of it." He also quotes the rhyme sailors knew in my time,

> "Old horse! Old horse what brought you here?"
> "From Sacarap to Portland Pier
> I carted stone for many a year!
> I labored long and well, alack,
> Till I fell down and broke my back.
> They picked me up with sore abuse
> And salted me down for sailors use.
> The sailors, they do me despise,
> They pick me up and damn my eyes,
> They eat my flesh and gnaw my bones
> And throw the rest to Davy Jones."

[5]Richard Runciman Terry, an English writer, has prepared a work on chanties with piano accompaniment, and states that chanties should be spelled as pronounced — *shanty,* and that there is no good reason why uneducated sailors should select the French way of spelling the word. His "theory advanced and equally convincing that because negroes in West Indian seaports moved huts and shantys with a rope and song, the word should be pronounced and spelled so," is about as erroneous as the time he gives, showing no pull on *Reuben Ranzo* (under "Shanty Forms") while the chanteyman is singing his solo.

Hoisting chanteys were never sung so. He also speaks of *What shall we do with a Drunken Sailor,* another hoisting chantey for light work, as follows:

"This fine tune — in the first mode — was always a great favourite and *mostly* used for windlass or capstan."

I do not know what his experience at sea has been, but I will leave it to any deepwater sailor, or I'll bet my old sou'wester that he never heard it sung on the t'gallant fo'c'sle at the windlass.

We also sang this chantey at the topgallant halliards, a lighter hoist, where the pull comes in twice as often as a song at the topsail halliards, thus:

Oh, *Ran*-zo *was* no *sail*-or, *Ran*-zo *boys,* oh, *Ran*-zo.

[6]Clark's *Clipper Ship Era* disputes this, saying, "The *Dreadnaught* sailed from New York, February 27, 1859, and from her log, on March 12th, the distance sailed from Sandy Hook to the Northwest Lightship, 3018 miles; passage 13 days, 8 hours, mean time. It was during this passage that the *Dreadnaught* is supposed to have

made the run from Sandy Hook to Queenstown in 9 days, 17 hours. Her log shows that 9 days, 21 hours from Sandy Hook, she was not within 400 miles of Queenstown."

[7]W. B. Whall, in his *Sea Songs and Shanties,* states, "This song was referred to by Marryat on a visit to America in the [eighteen] thirties, where he went as a passenger in a sailing ship."
Basil Lubbock in *Around the Horn Before the Mast* gives other words to *Sally Brown.*

[8]This chantey is of English origin but it was sometimes sung on American vessels. The same air appears in Tozer's *Sailor Songs.*

[9]Another version of this chantey is found in John Masefield's *Sailor's Garland.*

[10]The words to this chantey were taken in part from Miss Laura Smith's *Music of the Waters.* We sang similar words, winding up with the old set words, "And up aloft this yard must go, stretch her leech and leave it so."

[11] This air, *Good-bye Annie Darling,* is given in S. B. Luce's *Naval Songs,* but Sailor Jack sang the words more often to *Blow the Man Down* than to any other tune. It was often sung as a "rounder" in which every man selected a fish and sang his solo in turn, as a chanteyman. If he wasn't equal to something original, you might hear words as follows:
> The salmon comes next and I'm here right on time,
> But hell and damnation! I can't make a rhyme.

WHALING SONGS

[1]This song was sent to me by Mrs. Mary B. Plasket of Nantucket. Her grandfather, Captain Seth Pinkham, was master of the whaling ships *Galen* and *Dauphin,* in the year 1818.

[2]Capt. W. B. Whall states that he had forgotten the name of the captain in the song and took the name given by John Masefield; he also says that the old Scottish whalemen called the whale "whalefish" as did the Germans.

[3]*The Greenland Whale* was sung by Richard Duncan, a negro sailor. It shows how the negroes adapt the original to suit the occasion. He said it was sung this way as a capstan chantey by the negroes in the south.

[4]This song was given me by Capt. R. W. Nye, of the bark *Guy C. Goss,* who had seen service in early days on whalers.
Miss Colcord in her *Roll and Go* says: "I have been unable to find any who recalls the air to which this fine old song was sung. It was a favorite with the "bowhead" whalemen, who were accustomed to put in at Hawaiian Islands, on the homeward voyage, after a season in the Arctic."

INDEX OF FIRST LINES

INDEX OF FIRST LINES

INDEX OF SONG TITLES

247